Bugs of The Future Primitive:

A Colouring Book by Ian Piper

Pelekinesis

"Bugs of the Future Primitive: A Colouring Book" by Ian Pyper

ISBN: 978-1-938349-11-9

Illustrations and calligraphy by Ian Pyper
Layout and design by Mark Givens

Printed in the USA
First Pelekinesis Printing 2013

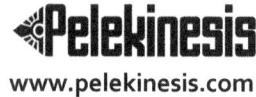
www.pelekinesis.com

"MAN IS AN ARTIFACT DESIGNED FOR SPACE TRAVEL. HE IS NOT DESIGNED TO REMAIN IN HIS PRESENT BIOLOGICAL STATE ANY MORE THAN A TADPOLE IS DESIGNED TO REMAIN A TADPOLE. "

WILLIAM S. BURROUGHS

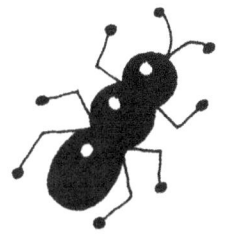

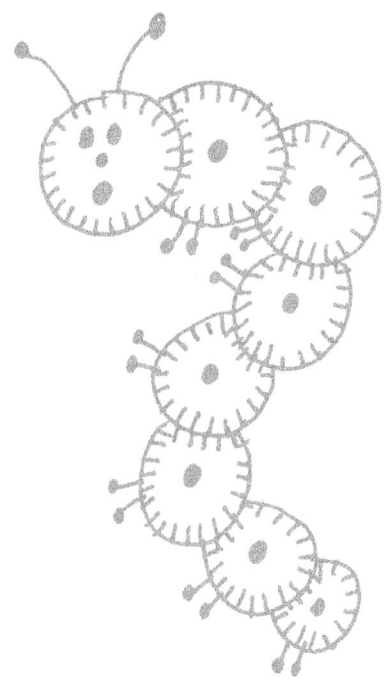

BUGS OF THE FUTURE-PRIMITIVE:

A COLOURING BOOK

IAN PYPER

THERE HAS BEEN A PARALLEL DEVELOPMENT IN HUMAN AND BUG SOCIETIES. BUGS CO-OPERATE ON BROOD CARE, HAVE DIVISION OF LABOUR AND CREATE HIVE COLONIES AND CITIES TO PROTECT AGAINST ENEMIES AND PROMOTE SURVIVAL STRATEGIES AGAINST THE VAGARIES OF THE WEATHER AND THE HARSHEST OF ENVIRONMENTS TO CREATE THEIR OWN ECOLOGICAL NICHES.

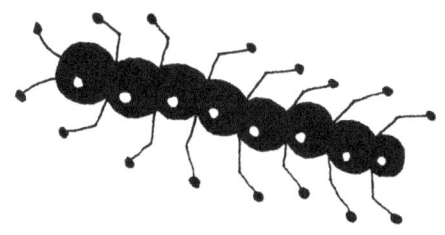

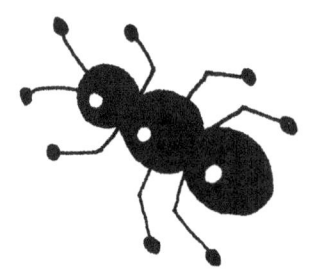

PSYCHOLOGIST AND WRITER TIMOTHY LEARY HAS LIKENED HUMAN BEINGS TO BUGS AND HAS SUGGESTED THAT HUMAN DEVELOPMENT IS ONLY THE LARVAL STAGE OF A MUCH LONGER EVOLUTIONARY CHAIN. IN THE SAME WAY THAT CATER-PILLARS DEVELOP INTO BUTTERFLIES, IT HAS BEEN SUGGESTED THAT HUMANS ARE MERELY PUPATING LARVAL EMBRYOS THAT WILL EVENTUALLY METAMORPHOSE, MUTATE AND EVOLVE FROM HUMAN THROUGH TRANS-HUMAN AND ON INTO POST-HUMAN CREATURES.

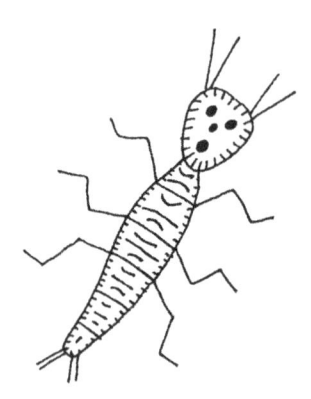

MUCH SPECULATION HAS BEEN MADE AS TO THE EVENTUAL FORM HUMAN BEINGS MAY TAKE (INCLUDING THE HYBRIDISATION OF SPECIES THROUGH GENE POOL GENETIC MODIFICATION, SPLICED DNA AND CLONING), BUT IT'S PERHAPS NOT TOO FAR FETCHED TO SUGGEST THAT THE PARALLEL DEVELOPMENT WITH BUGS MAY CONTINUE IN THE COMING CENTURIES AND POST-HUMANS MAY VERY WELL COME TO RESEMBLE A WHOLE RANGE OF INSECTOID-LIKE CREATURES PERFECTLY ADAPTABLE TO THE CHANGING AND CHALLENGING ECOLOGICAL ENVIRONMENTS THAT THEY MIGHT FIND THEMSELVES PRESENTED WITH.

THE FUTURE REALITY MAY VERY WELL BE BUG-SHAPED AND FUTURE URBAN CONSTRUCTIONS AND CITIES AND ITS POLITICS MAY DEVELOP MORE LIKE THE ORGANIC BUG COMPLEXES OF BEE, WASP AND ANT COLONIES OR HIVES AND FROM WHICH THE NEW POST-HUMANOID CREATURES MAY EVENTUALLY EMERGE.

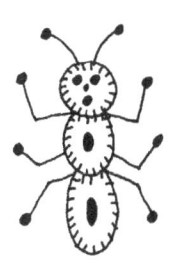

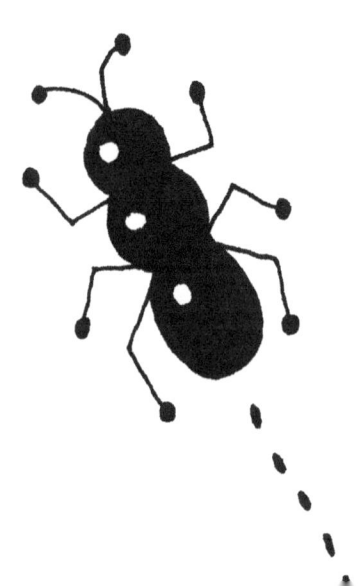

JOIN OUR INSECT NATION!

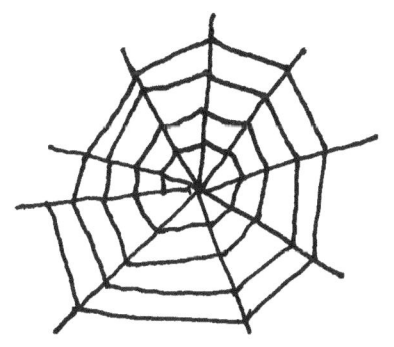

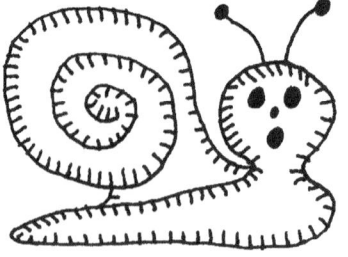

CITIES AS BUG HIVES AND COCOON CULTURE COLONIES, ORGANIC CELLULAR SOCIO-BIOLOGICAL SUBWAY TUBE CITIES, METROPOLISES AND COMPLEXES OF INSECTOID/HUMANOID/TRANS-HUMANOID/POST-HUMANOID CREATURES THAT ARE DIVERSE IN THEIR UNITY OF FUNCTION AND PURPOSE. CREATING A NEW HARMONY OF NEW ECOLOGIES AND BIOLOGICAL TECHNOLOGIES ....

...... BUGS ARE US!

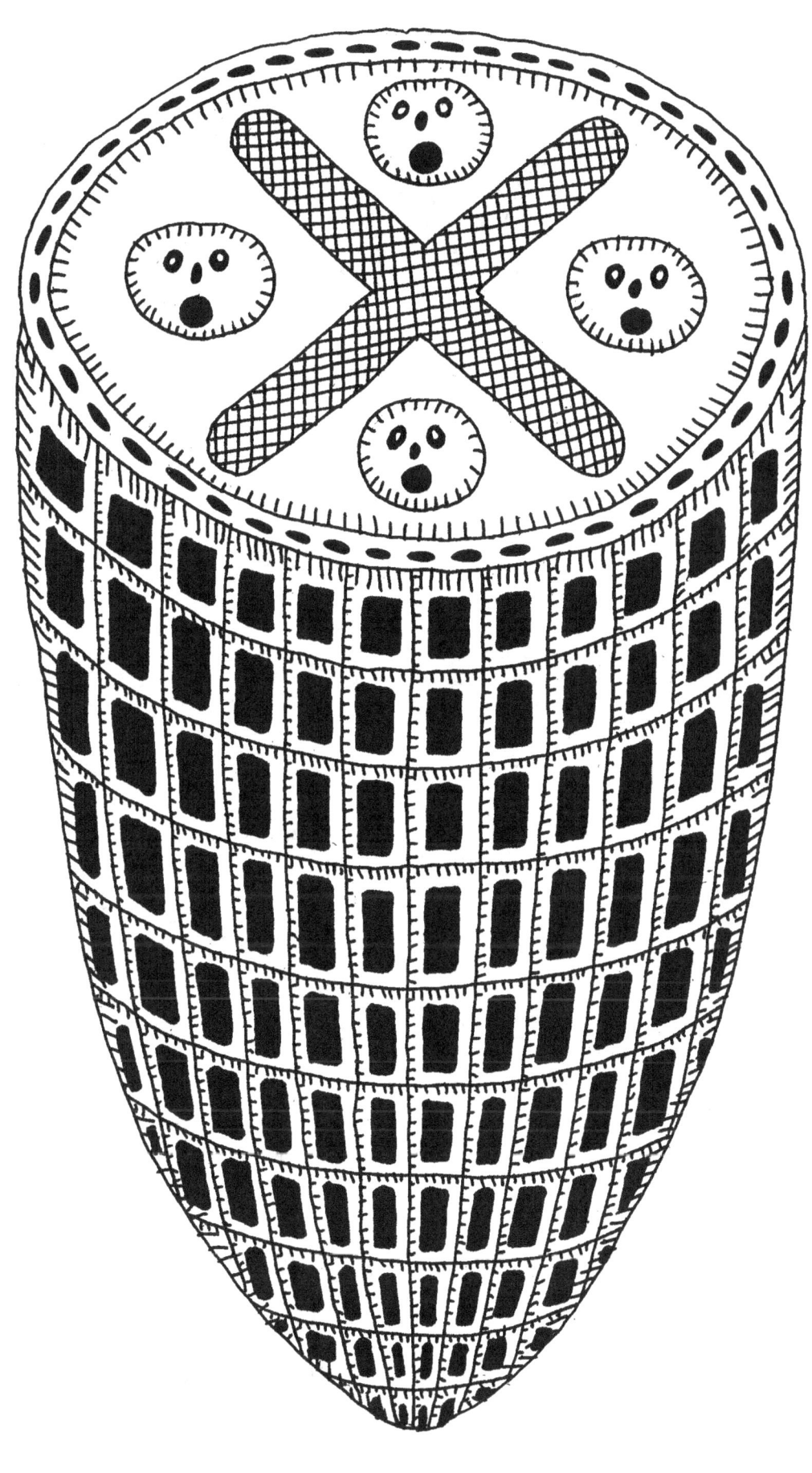

COLONY CROSS-SECTION

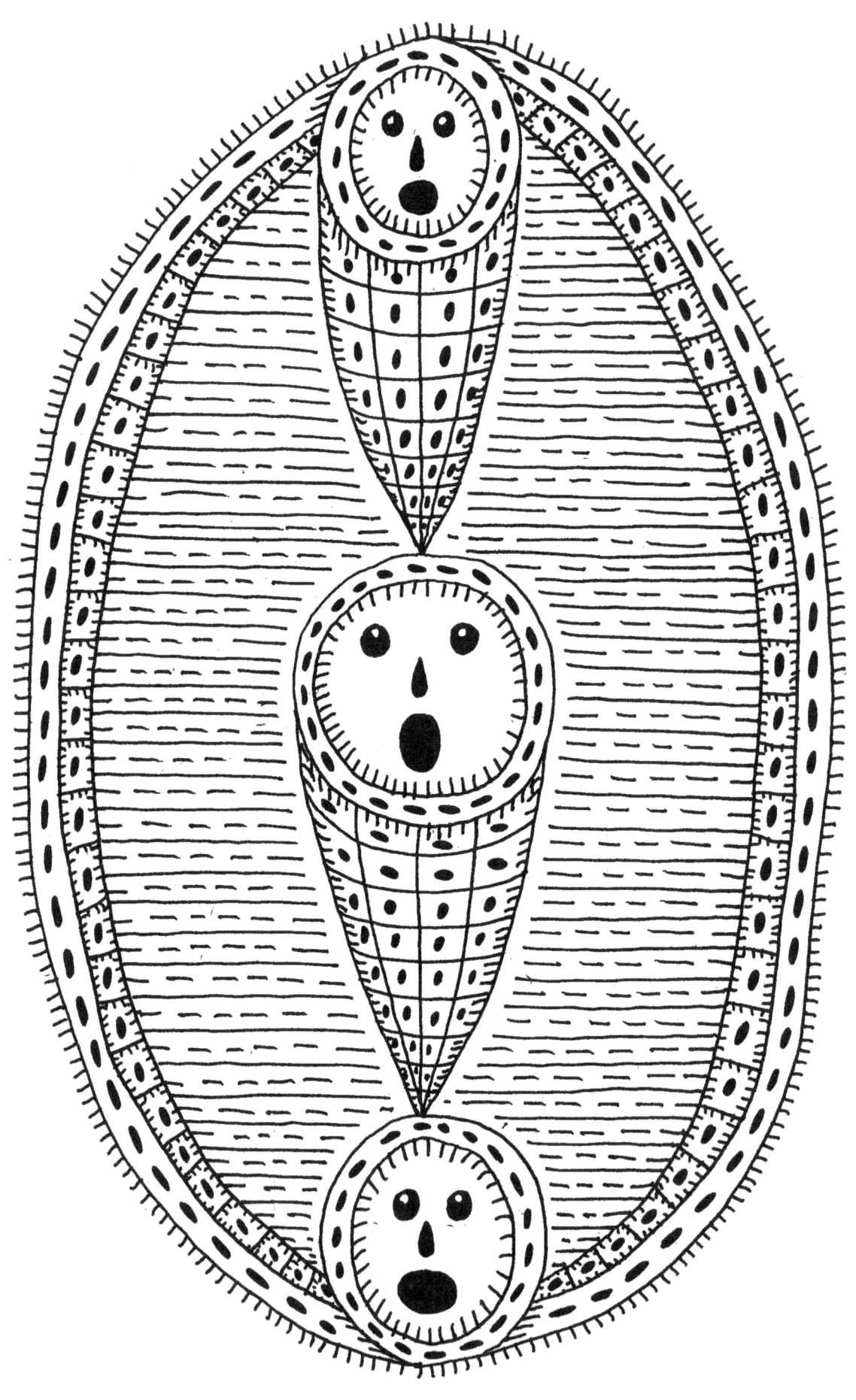

LARVAL BALANCE

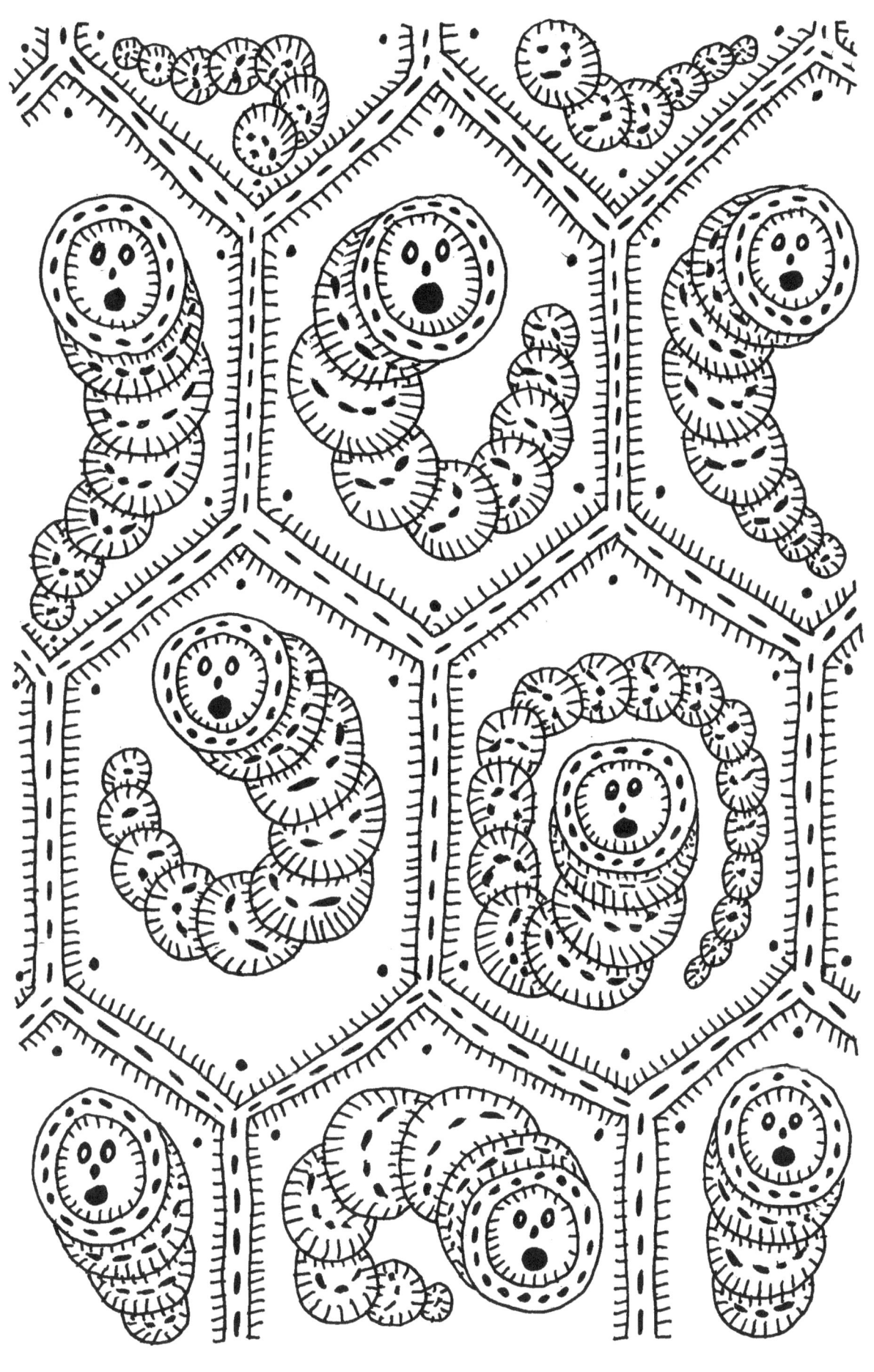

LARVAL COCOON HIVE

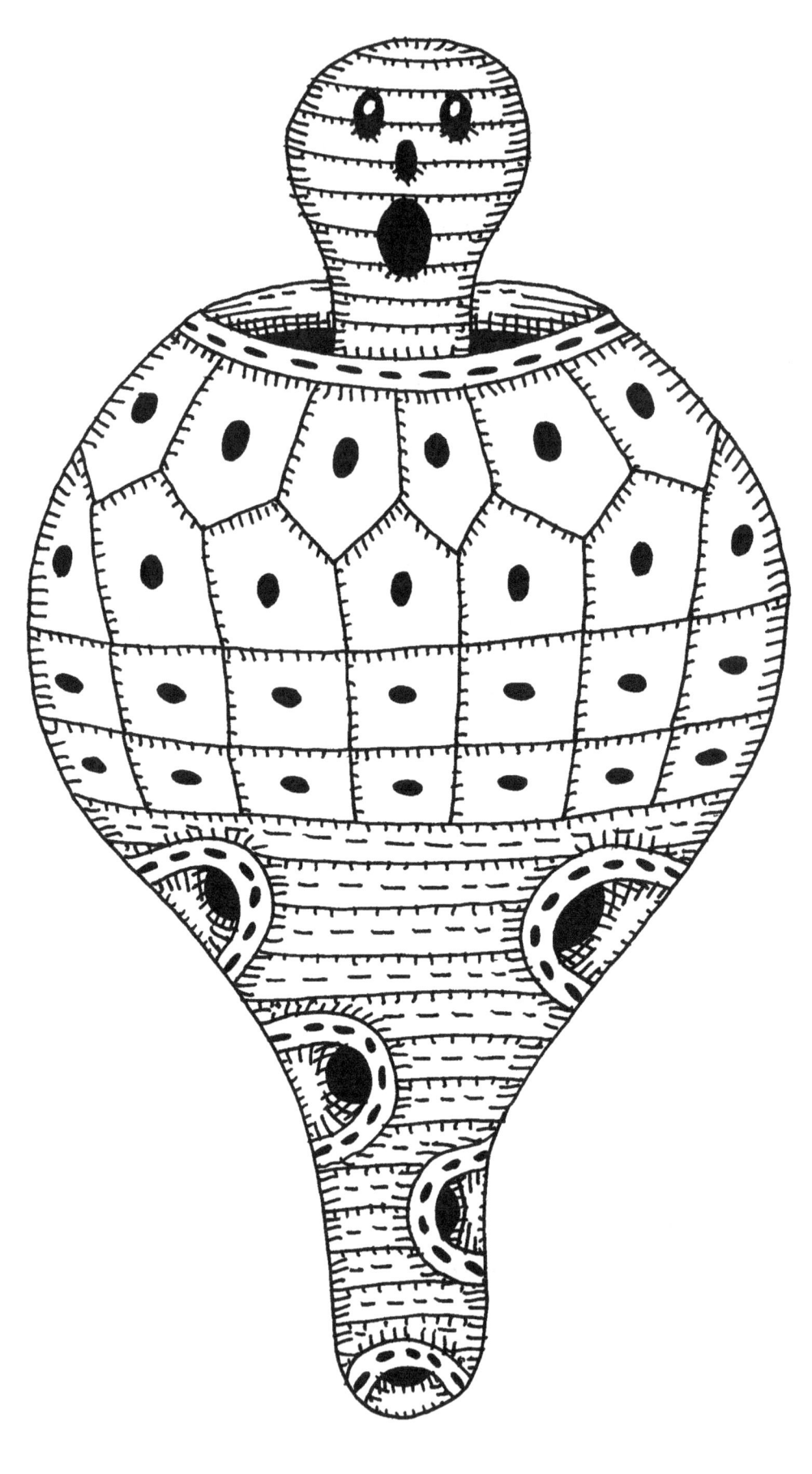

LARVAL COCOON LAYERS

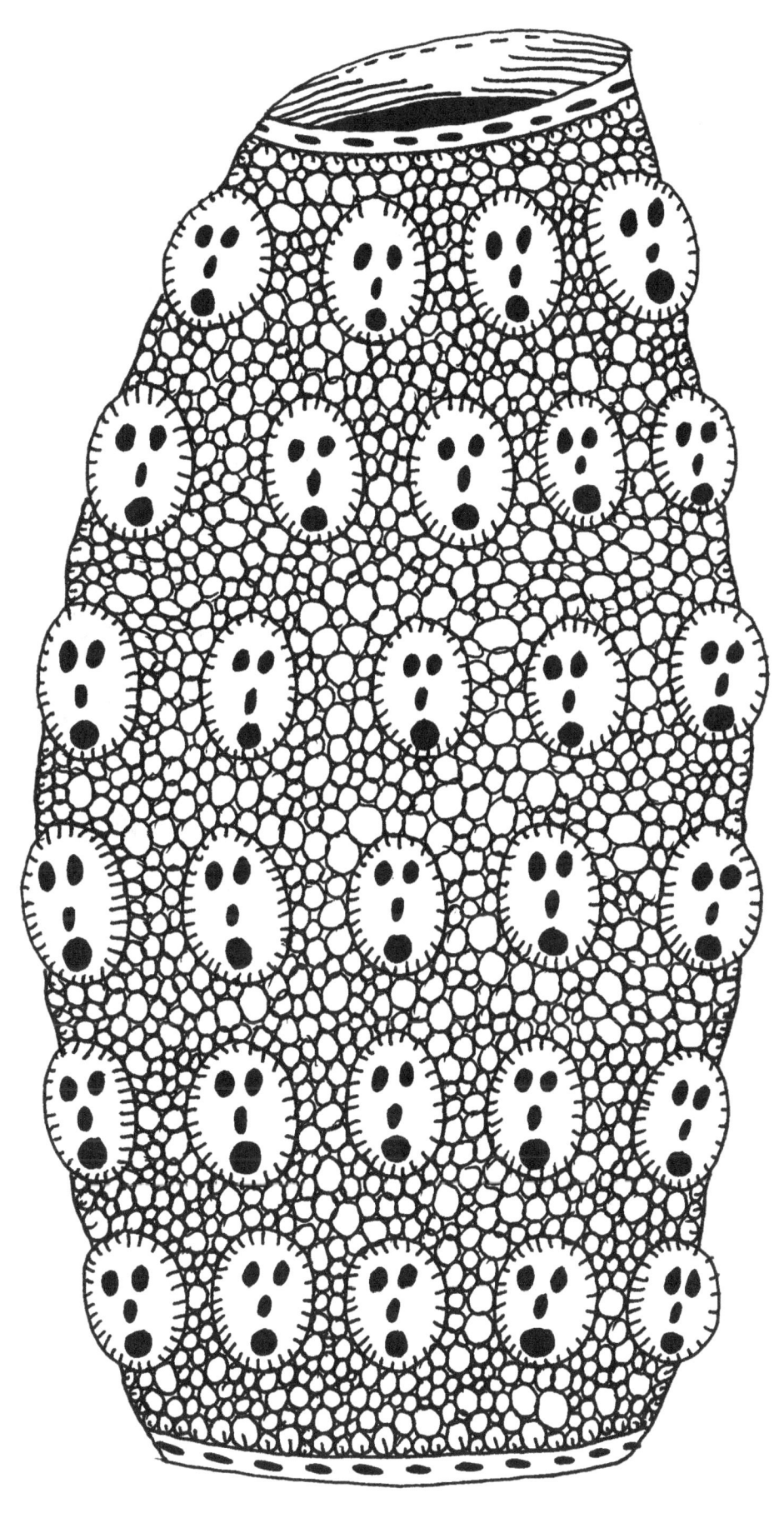

LARVAL COLONY STRUCTURE

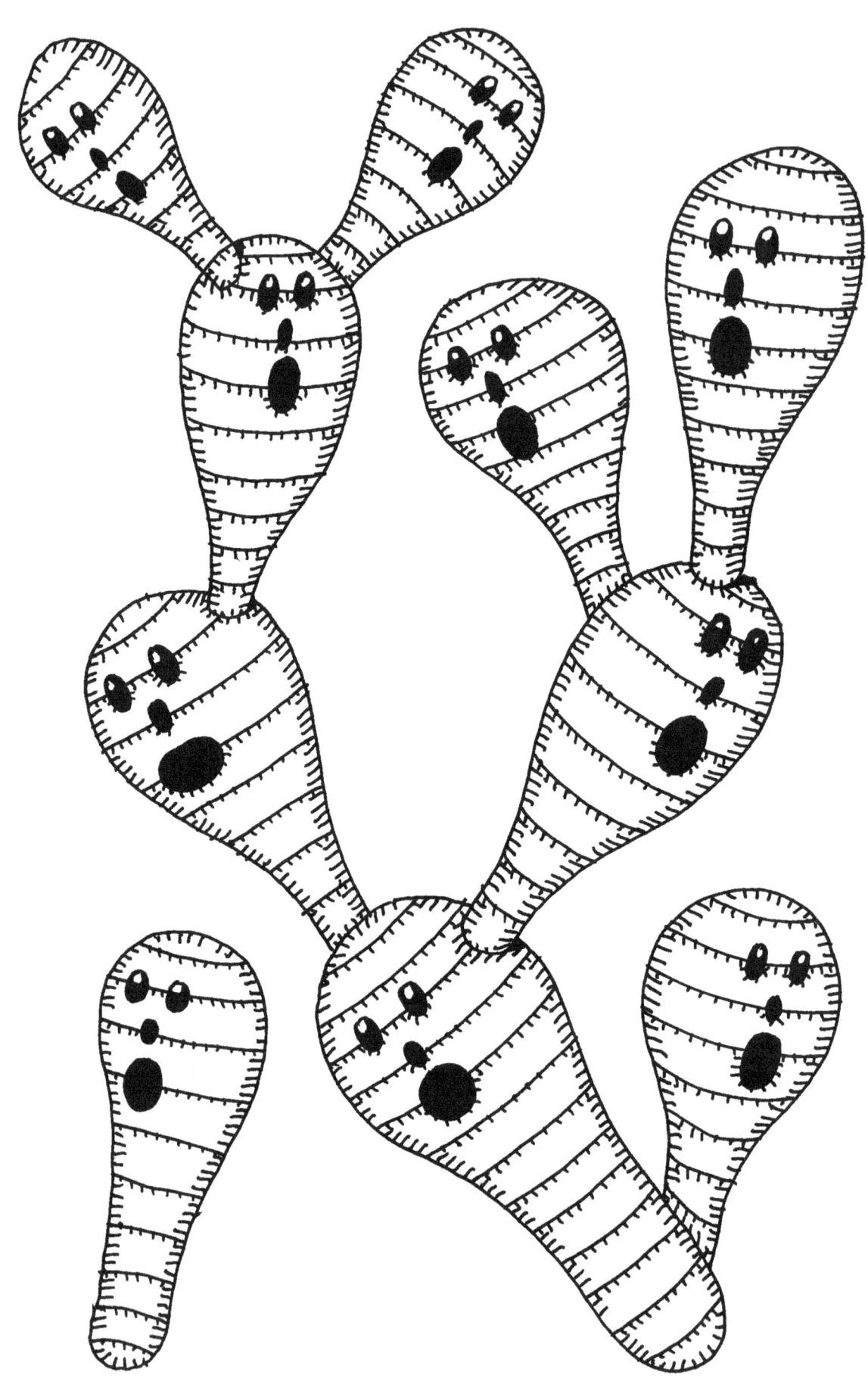

LARVAL POD COLONY

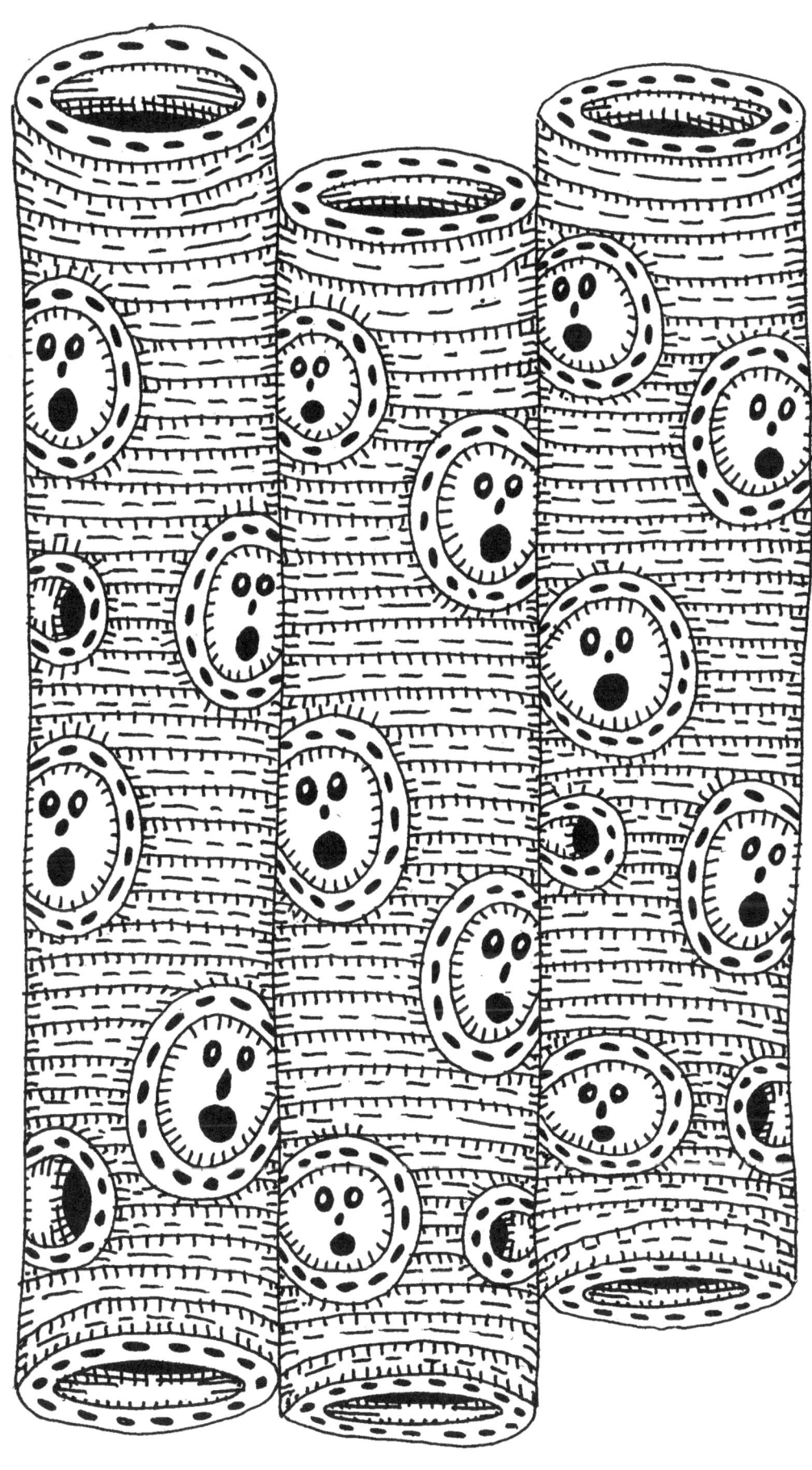

LARVAL TUBE STRUCTURES

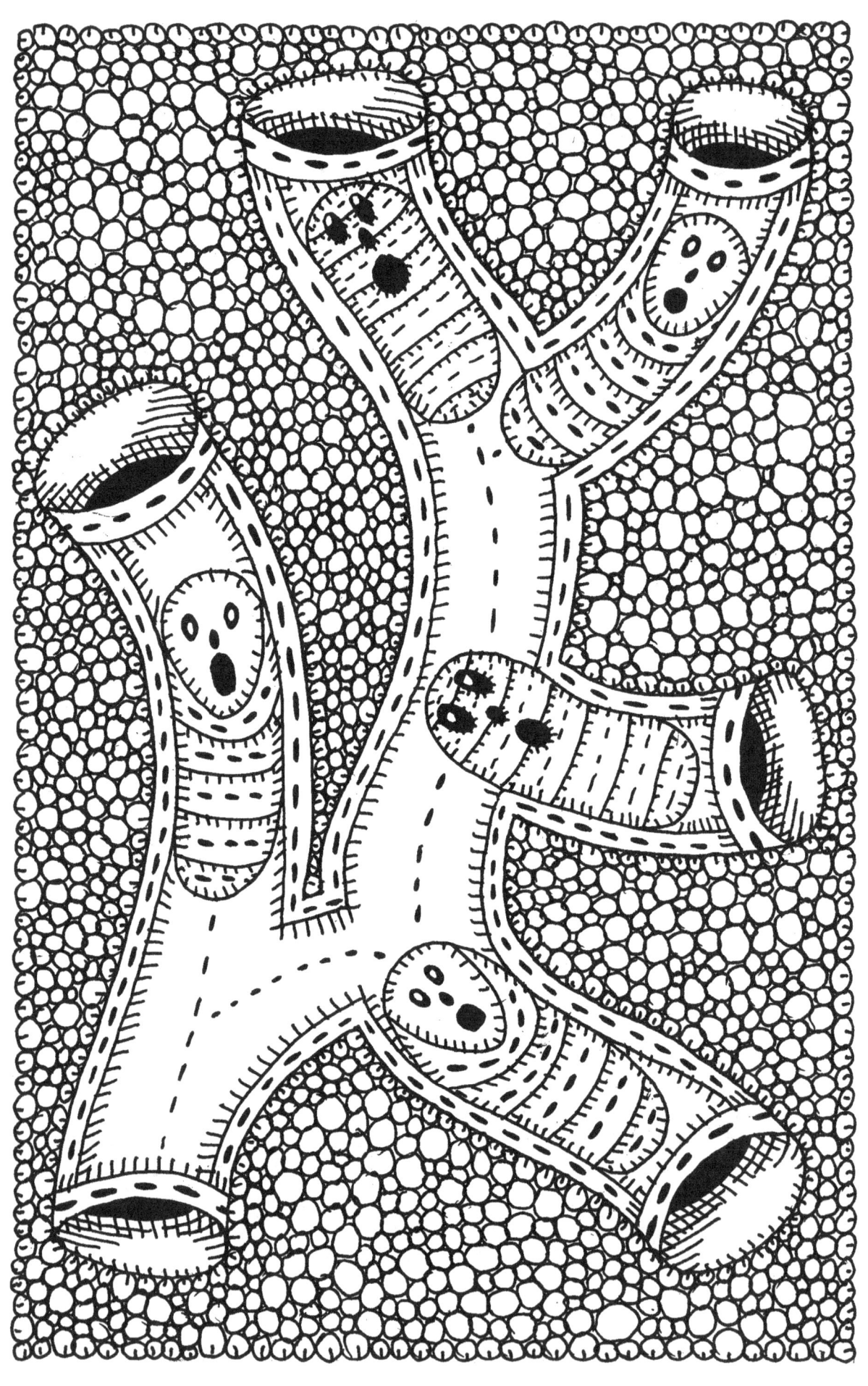

LARVAL TUBE TRANSPORT

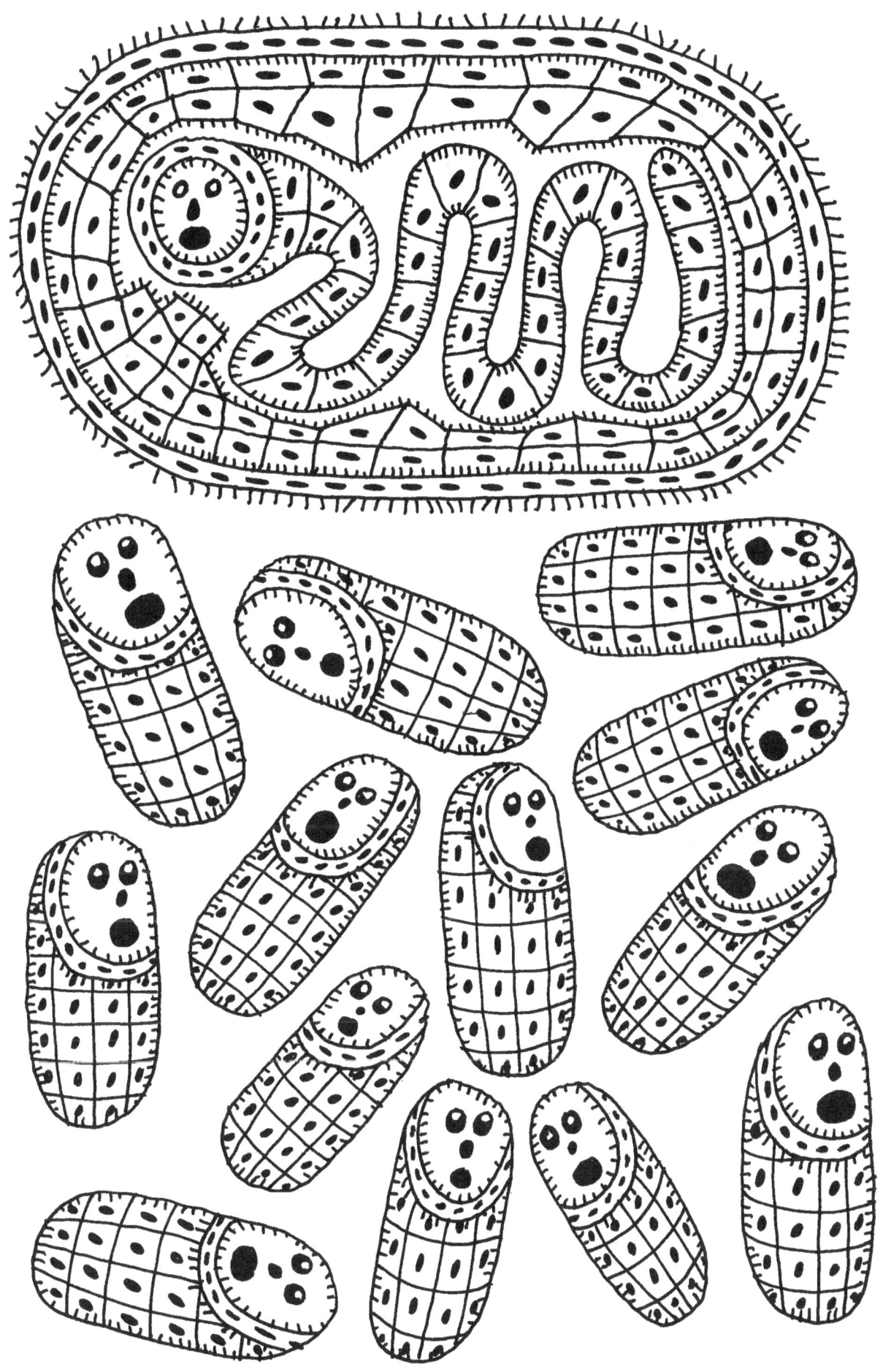

LOOSE COLONY

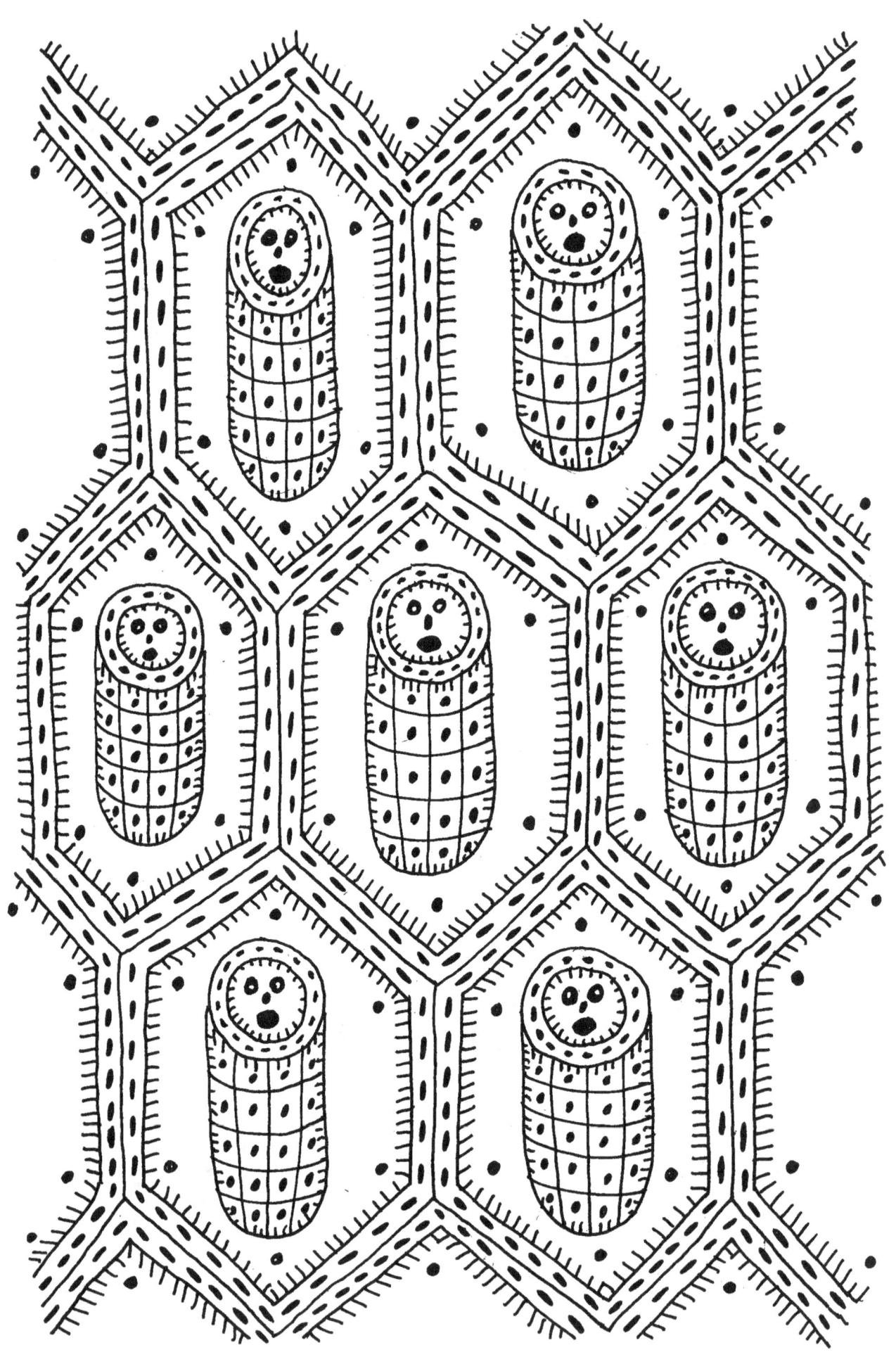

MAGGOT BABY HIVE

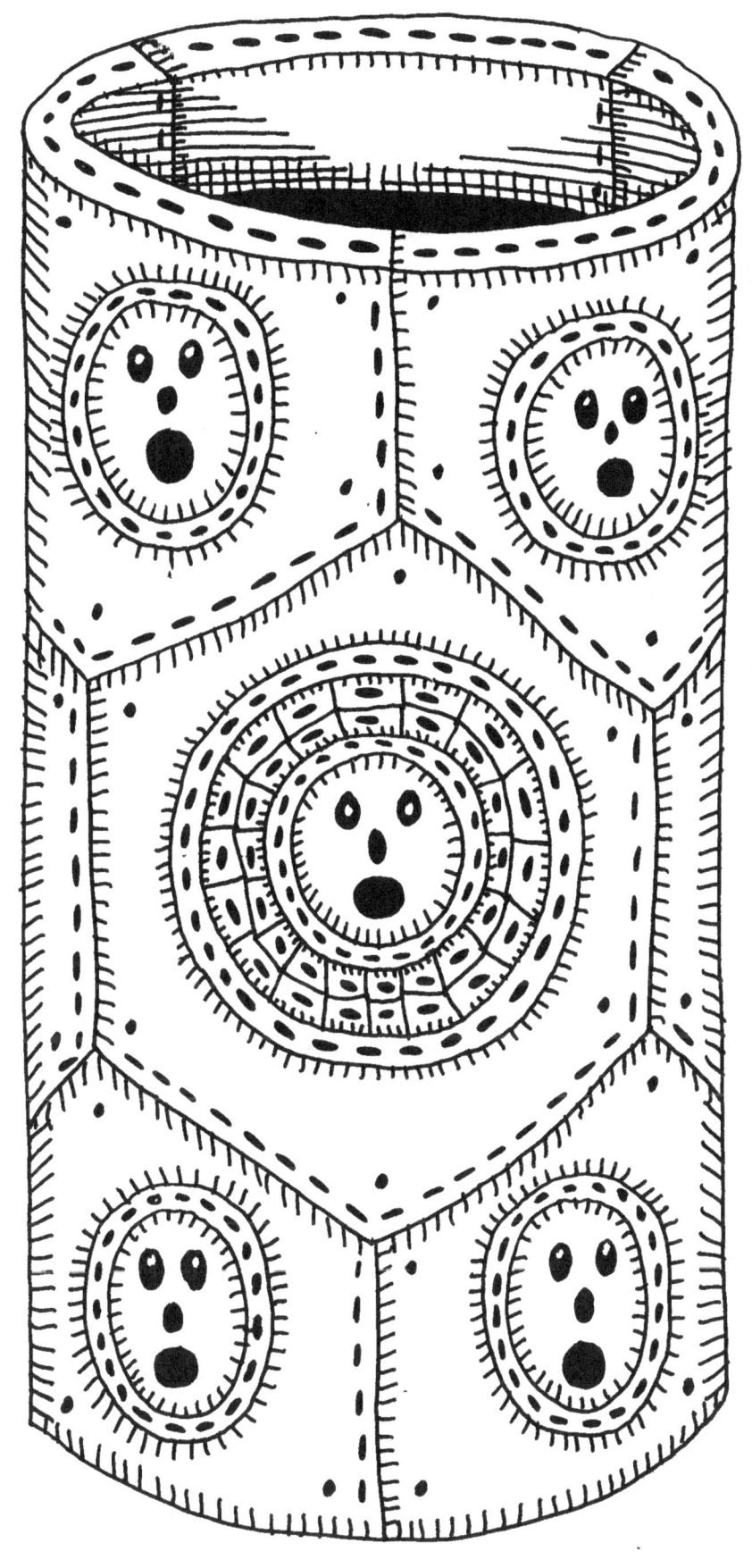

TUBE CELL COLONY

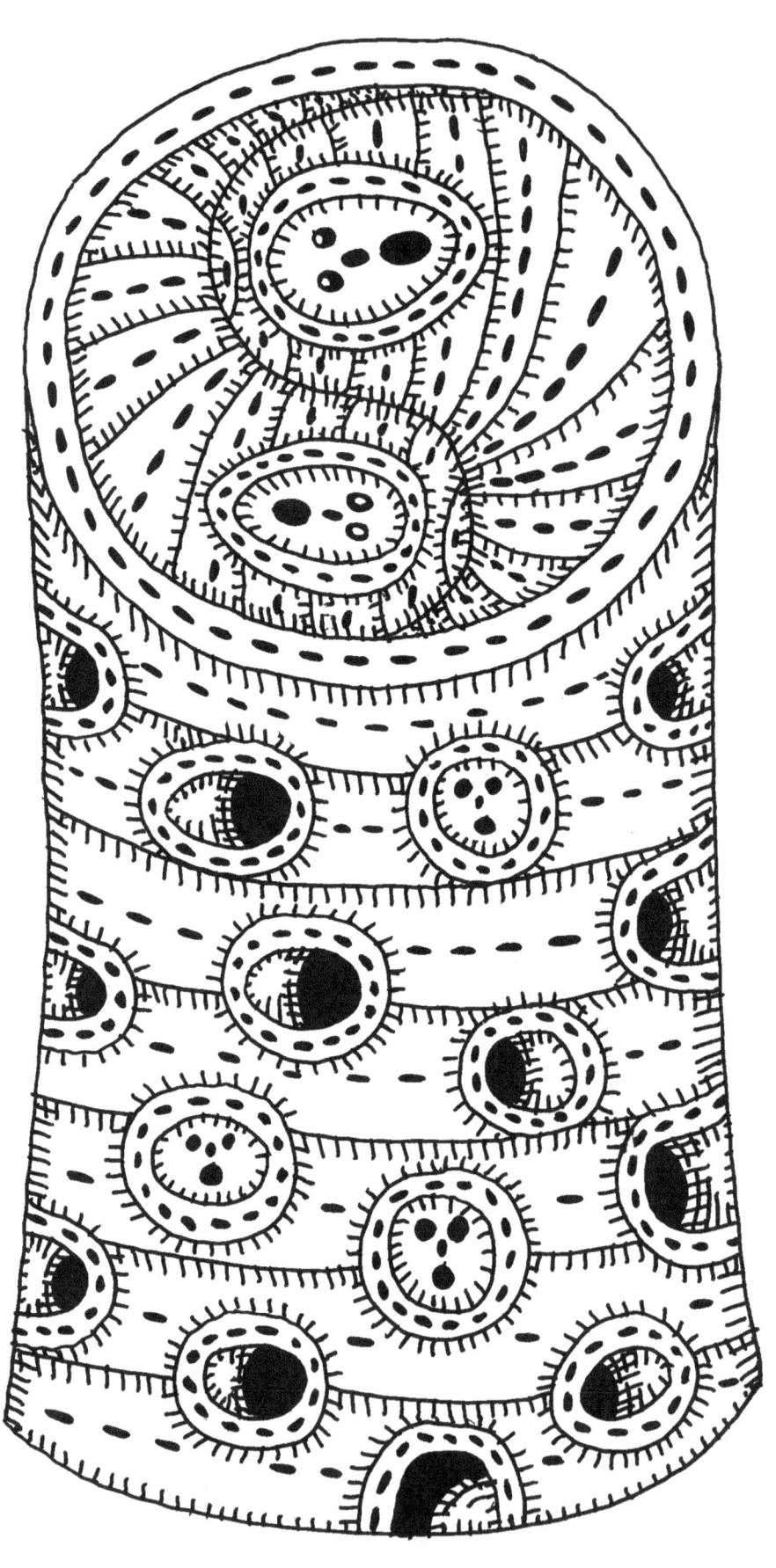

TUBE COLONY

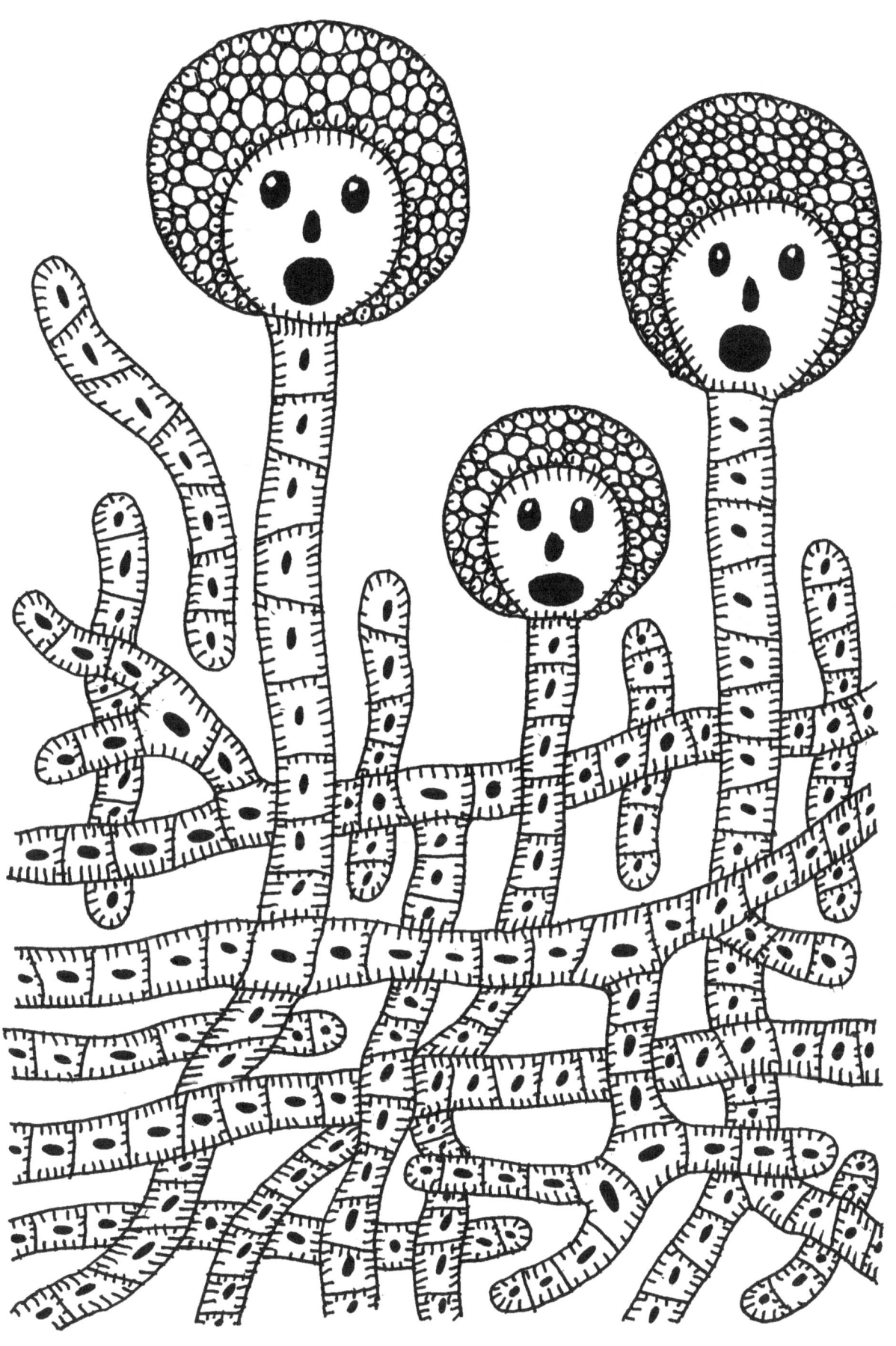

WORM CELL MATRIX

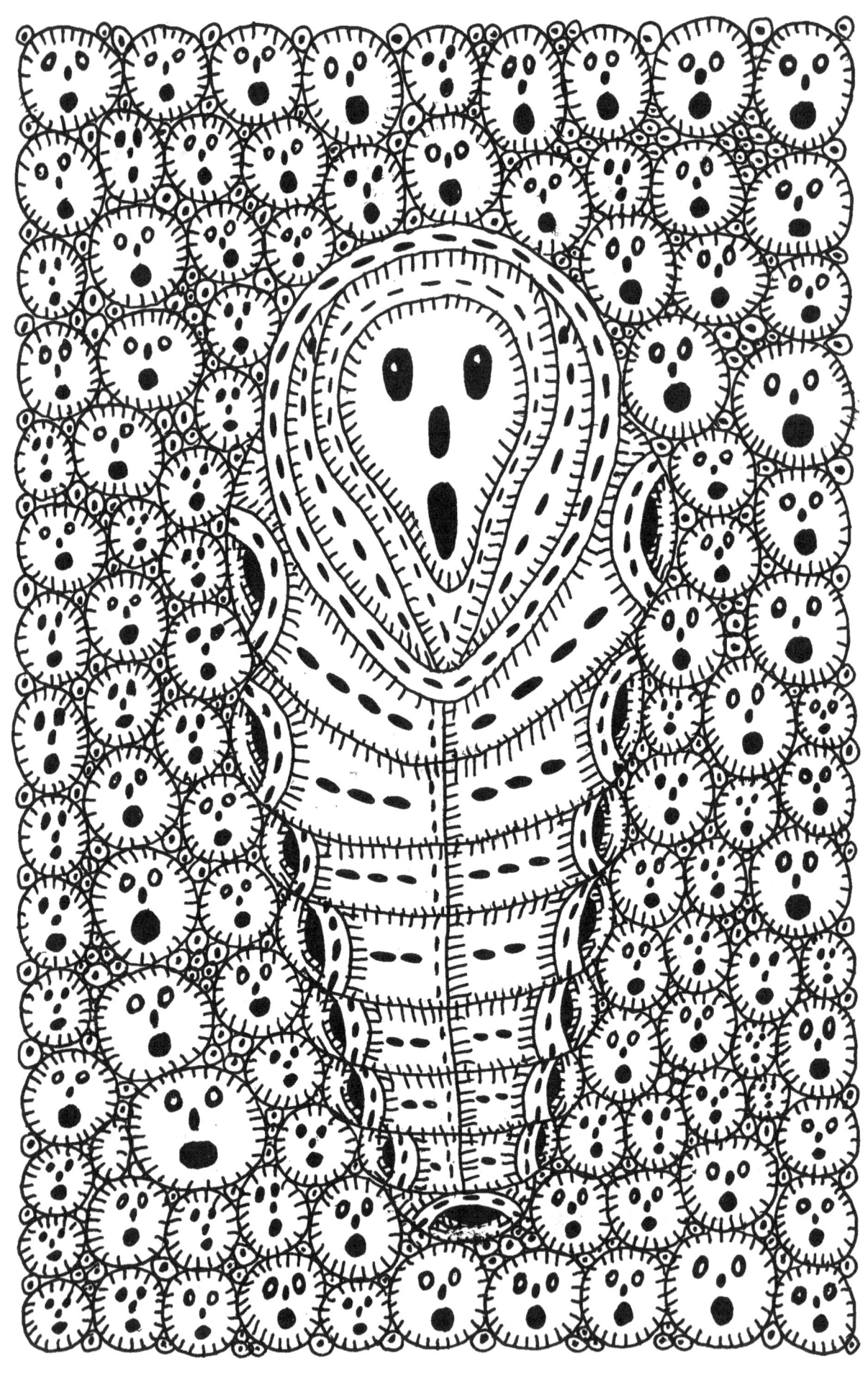

LARVA COLONY QUEEN

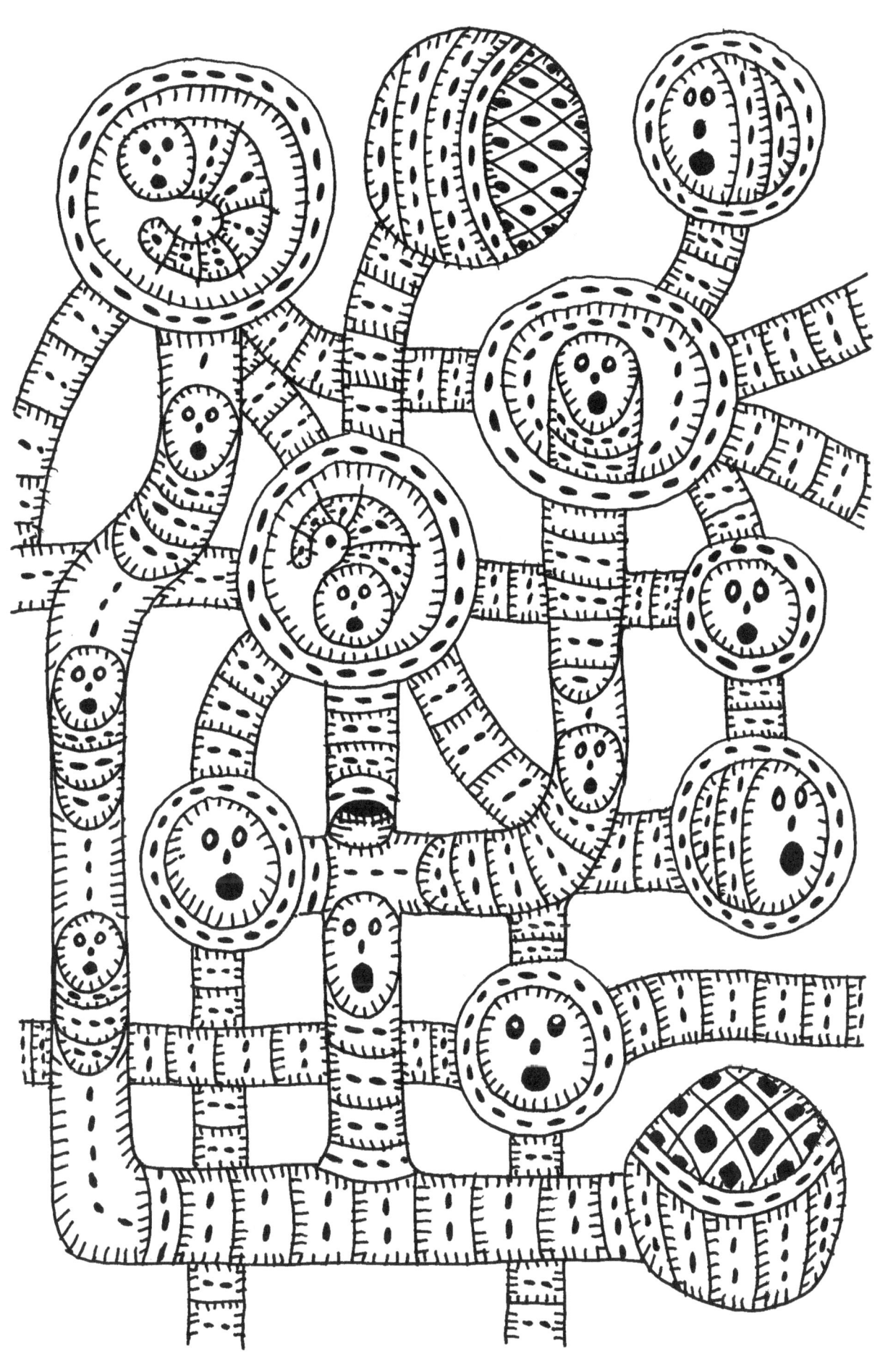

TUBE COLONY MATRIX

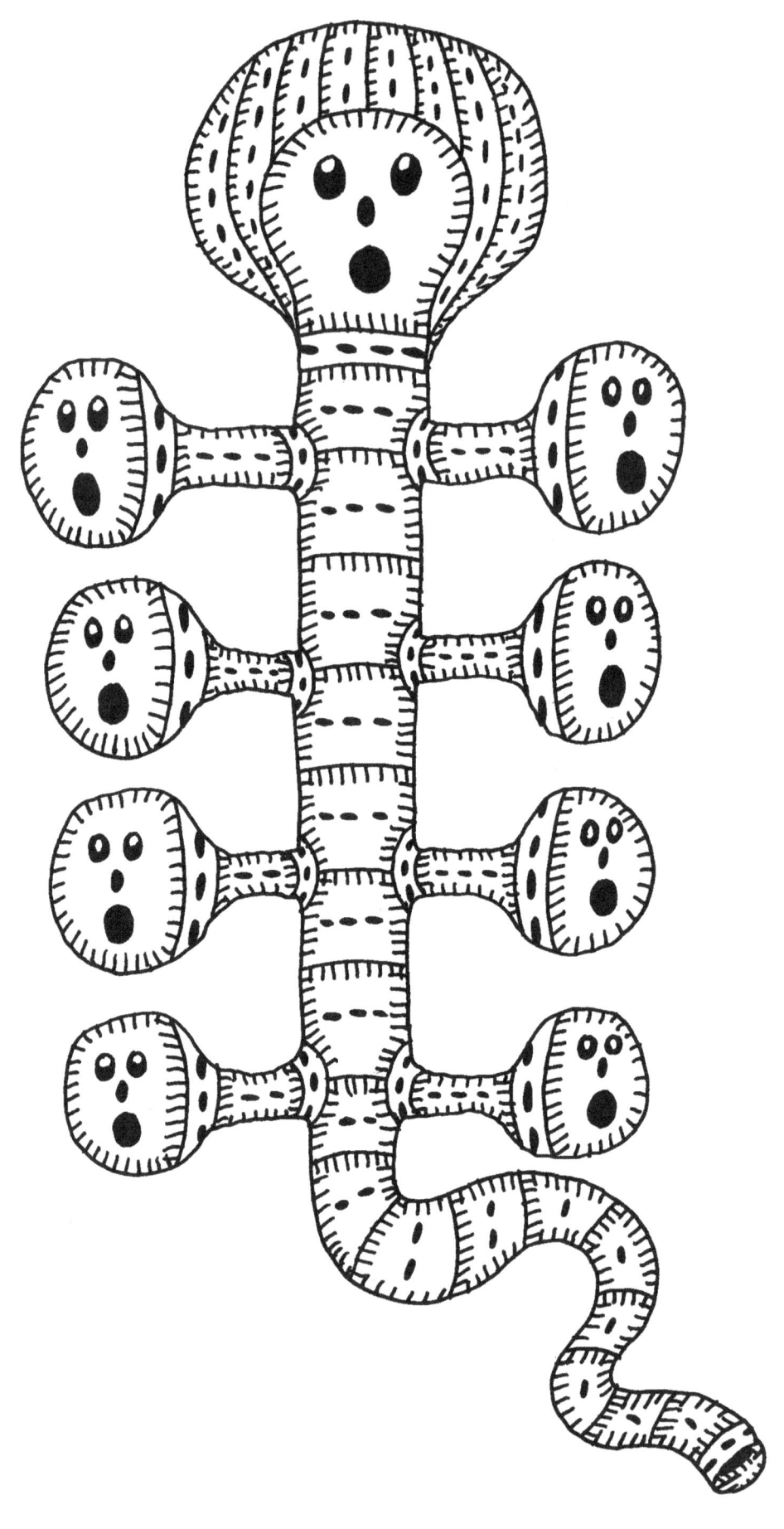

TUBE-WORM COLONY

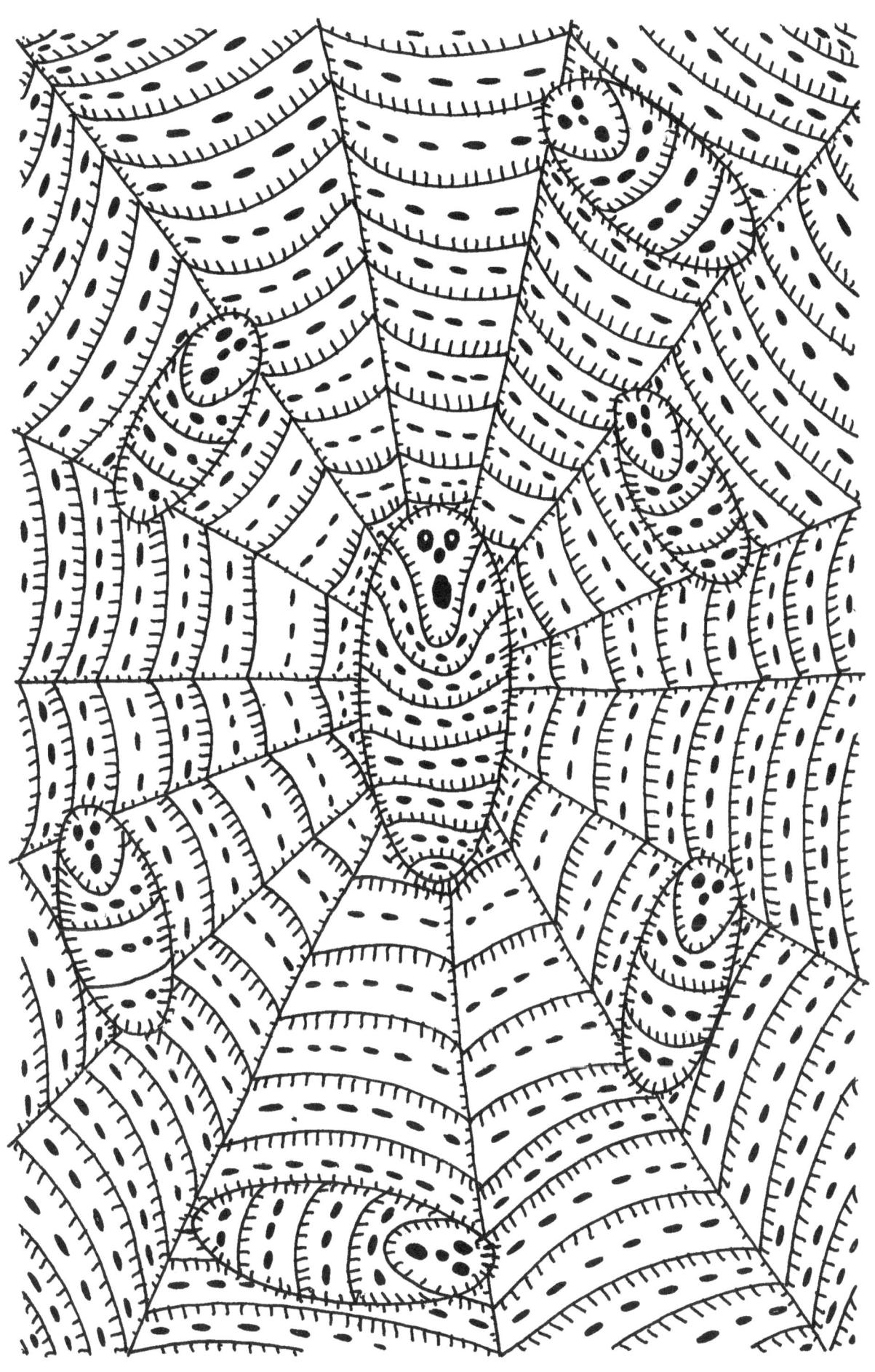

WEB LARVAE

THINGS THAT CRAWL THAT OUGHT TO WALK:
LEARN TO LOVE THE BUG IN US!

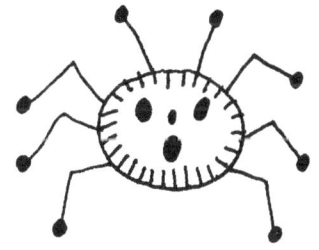

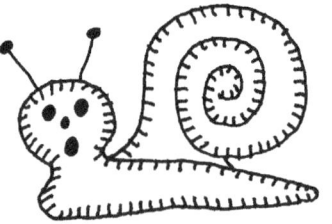

THE FUTURE WORLD OF EVOLVING GENETICALLY MODIFIED, GENE-SPLICED INSECTOIDS, HUMANOIDS, TRANS-HUMANOIDS AND POST-HUMANOIDS, ADAPTING THEMSELVES AND CREATING A WHOLE RANGE OF ECOLOGICAL ENVIRONMENTS AND NICHES. THE BUG MIND MODIFIED AND MELDED INTO THE DNA OF HUMANOIDS (AND VICE VERSA)

.....RISE BUG NATION!

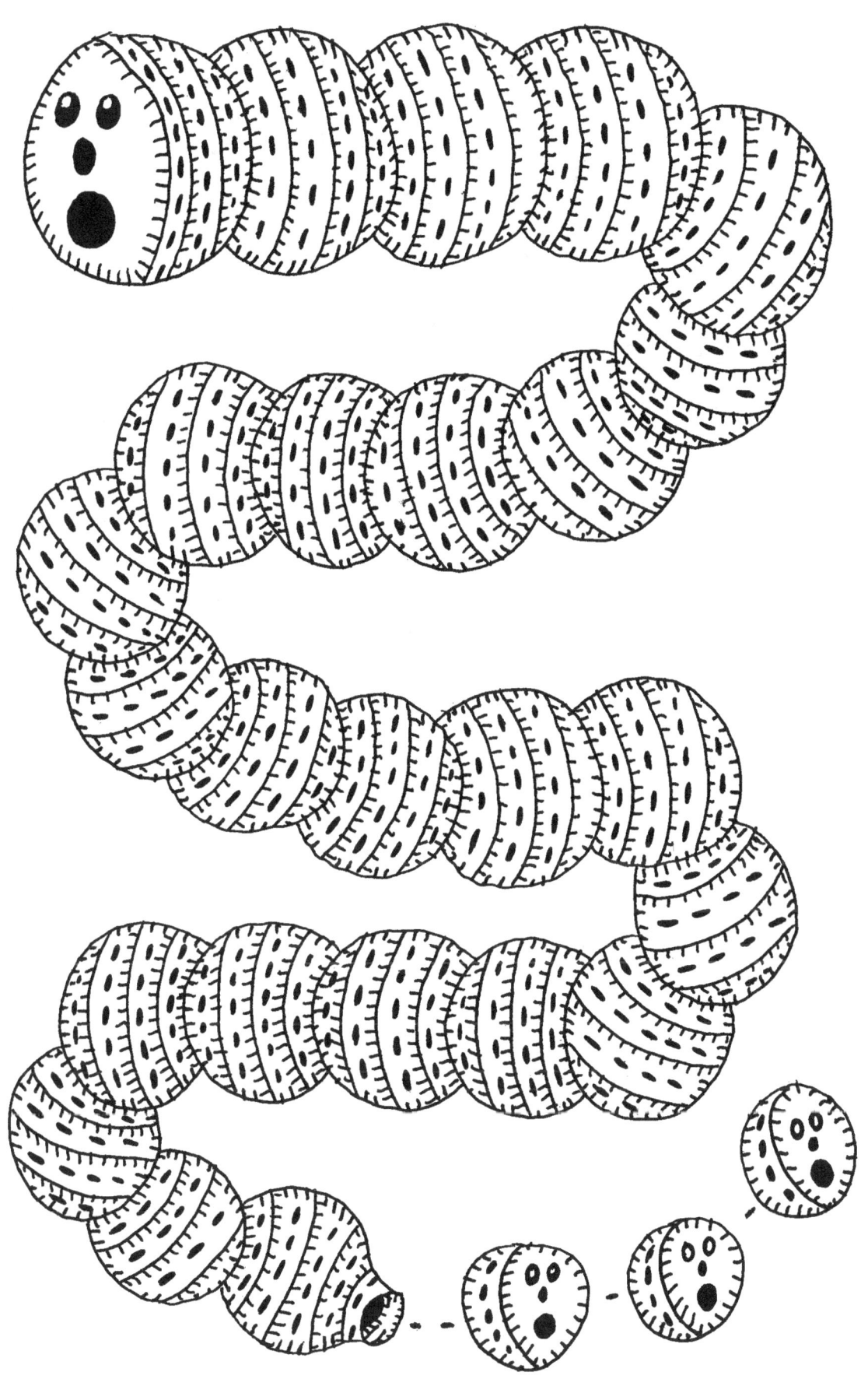

BIG WORM BIRTH

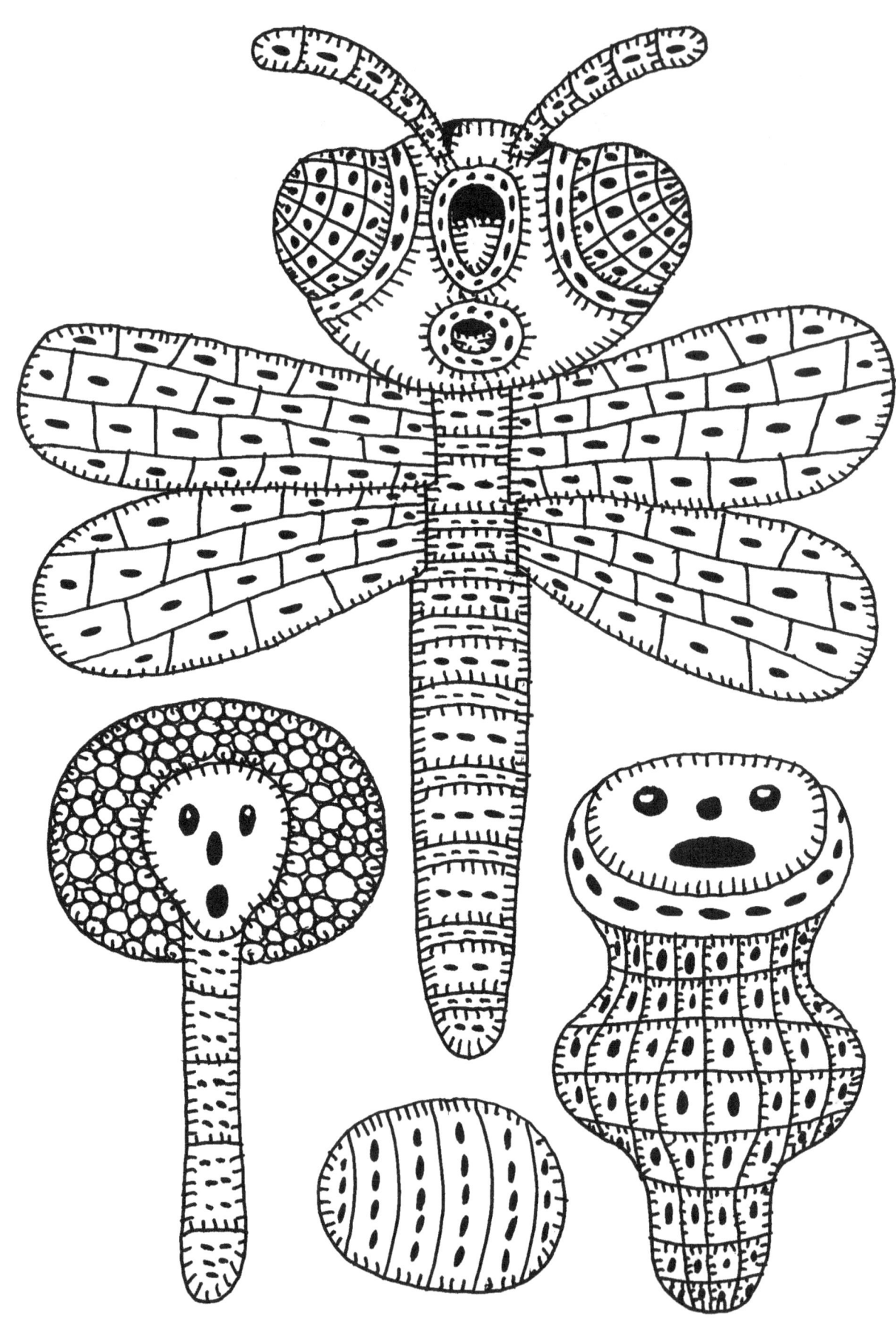

BUG ADAPTATIONS

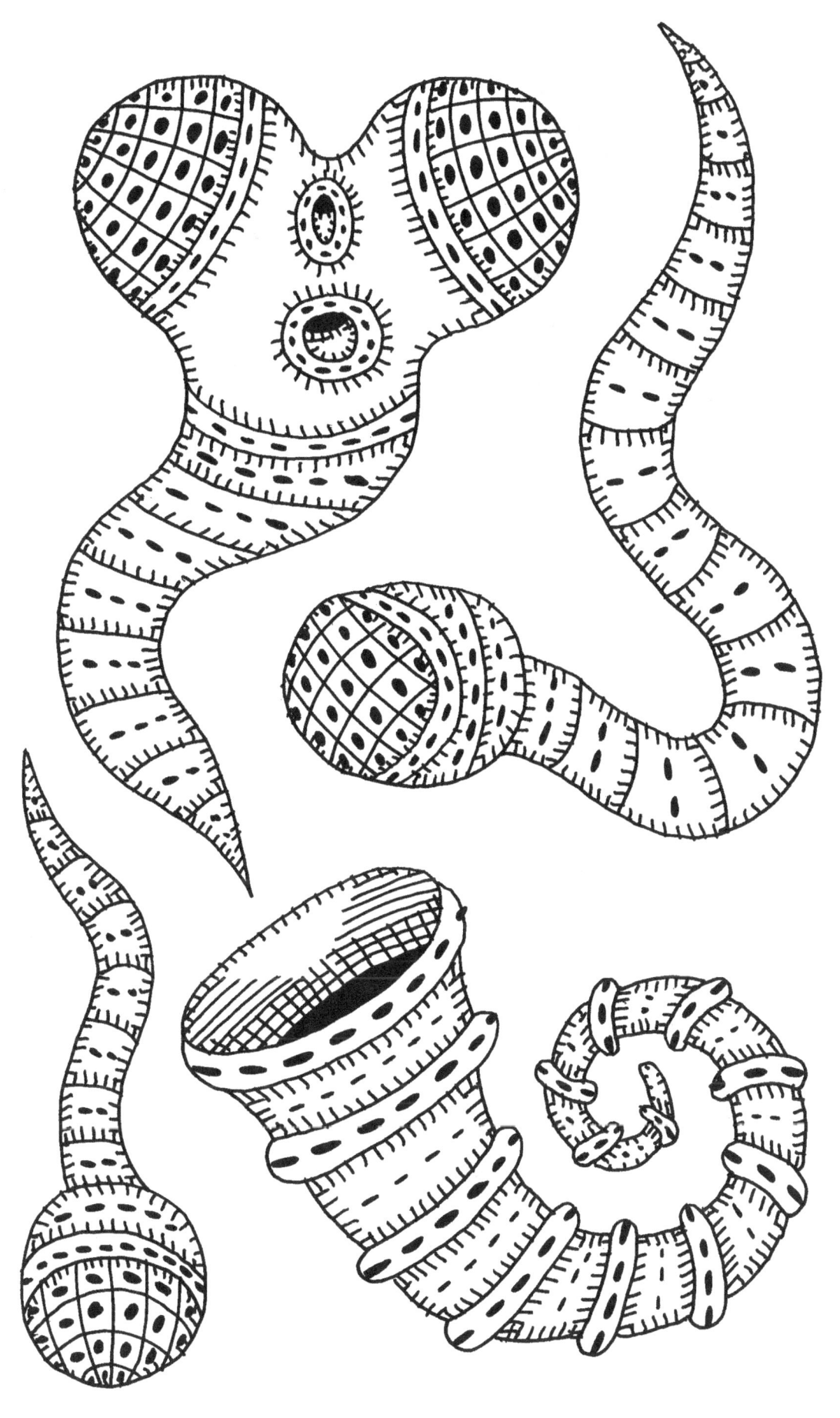

BUG ADAPTATIONS #2

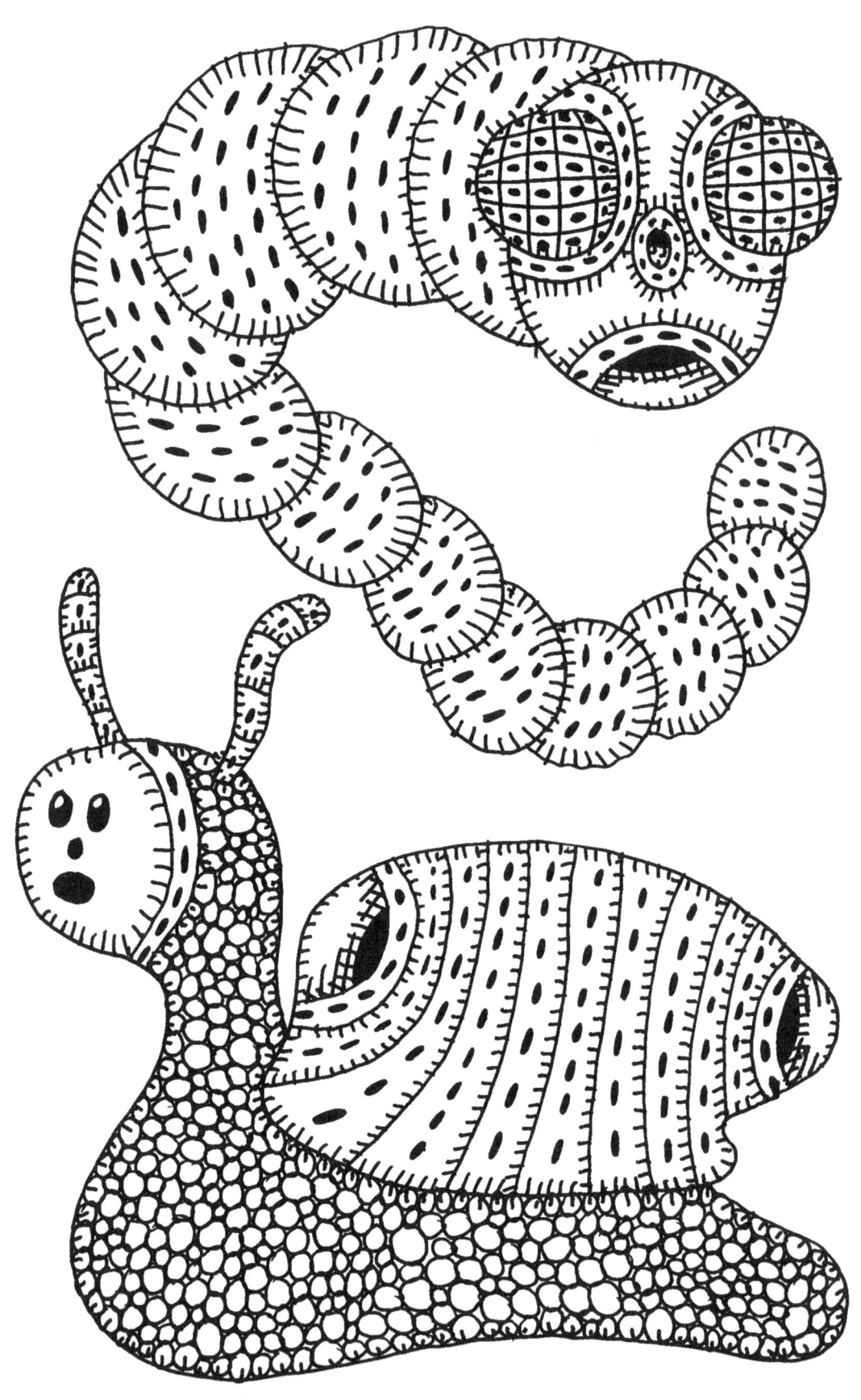

BUG MUTATIONS

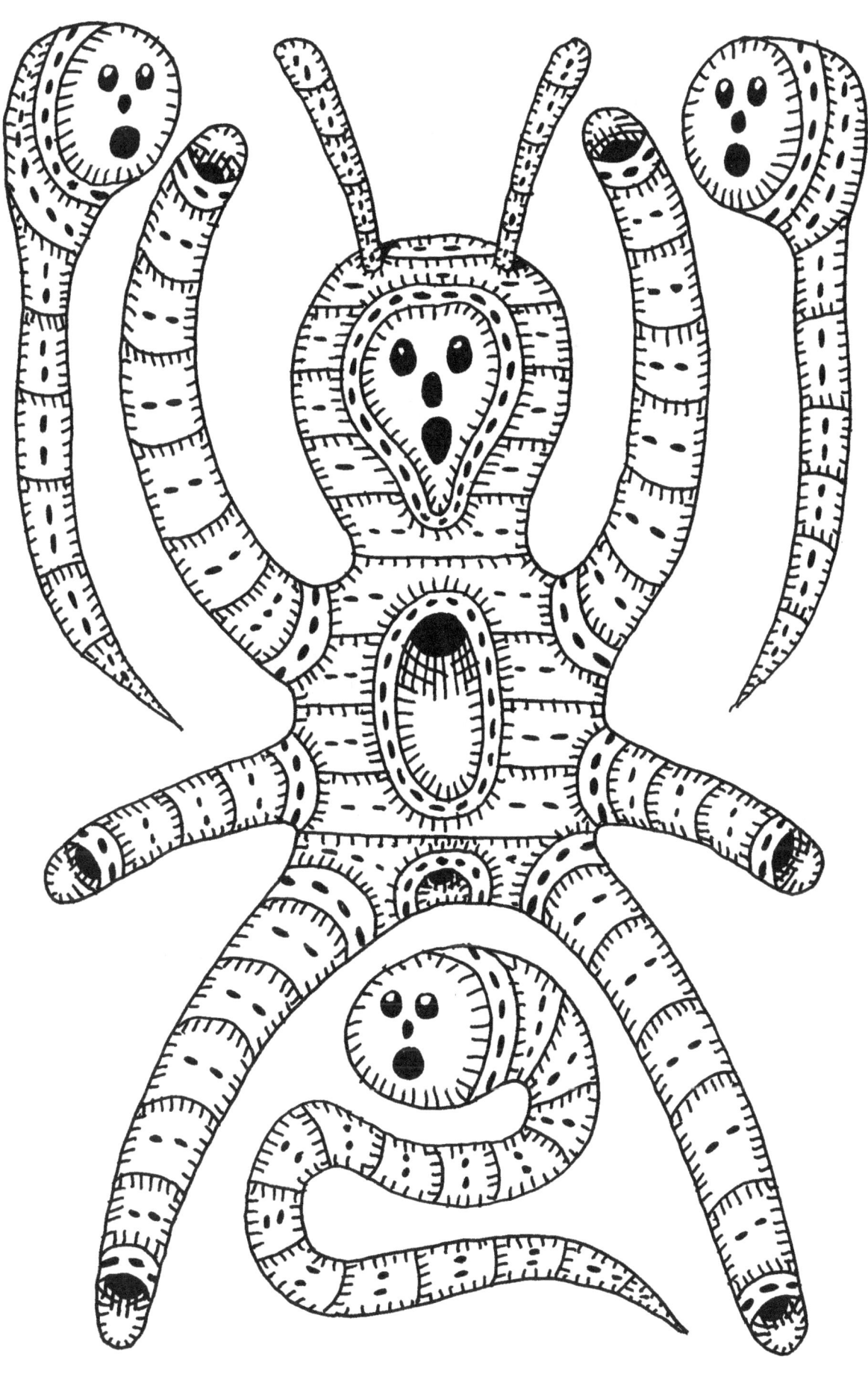

BUG MUTATIONS #2

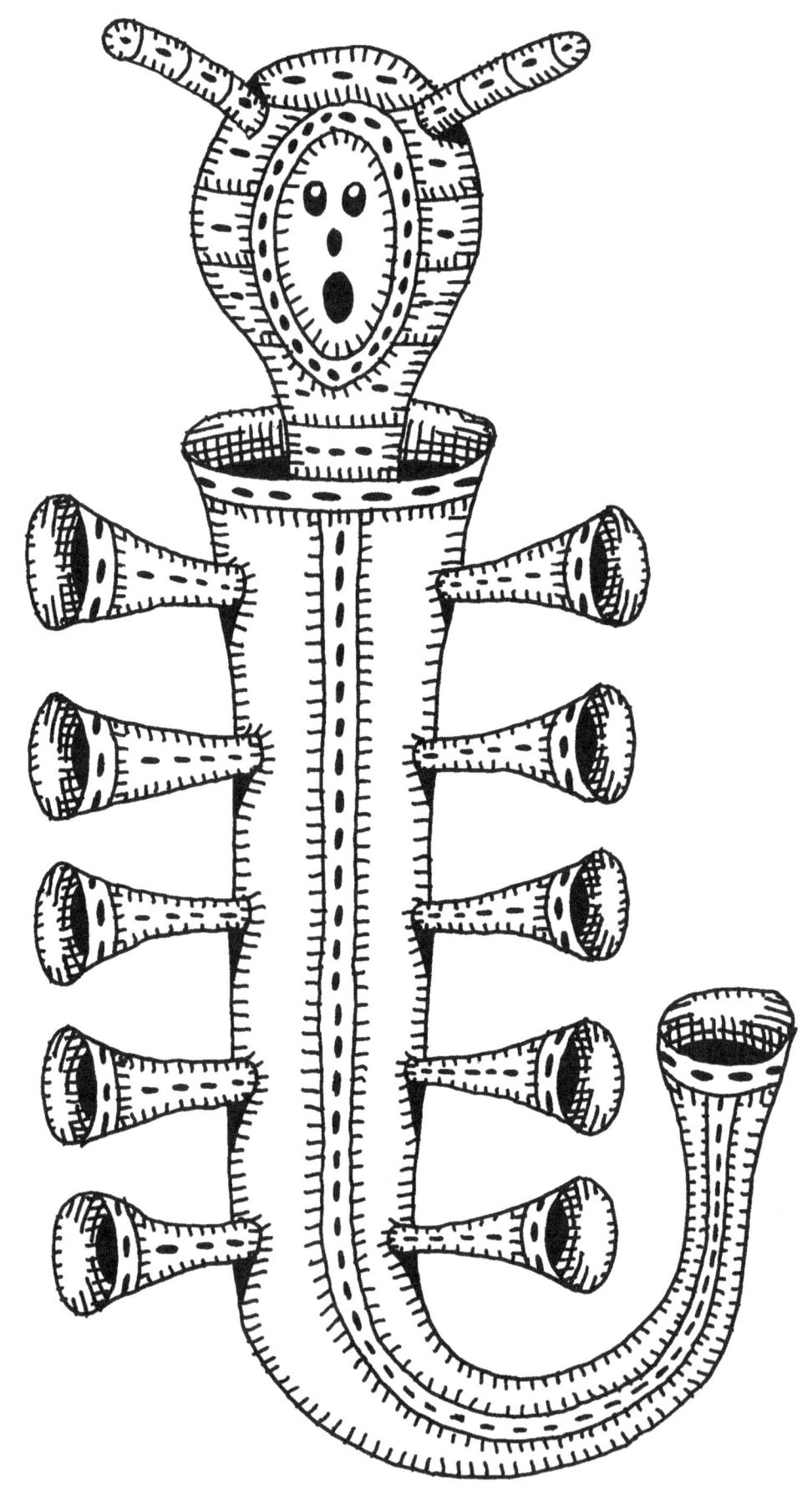

BUG BREATHING MECHANISM

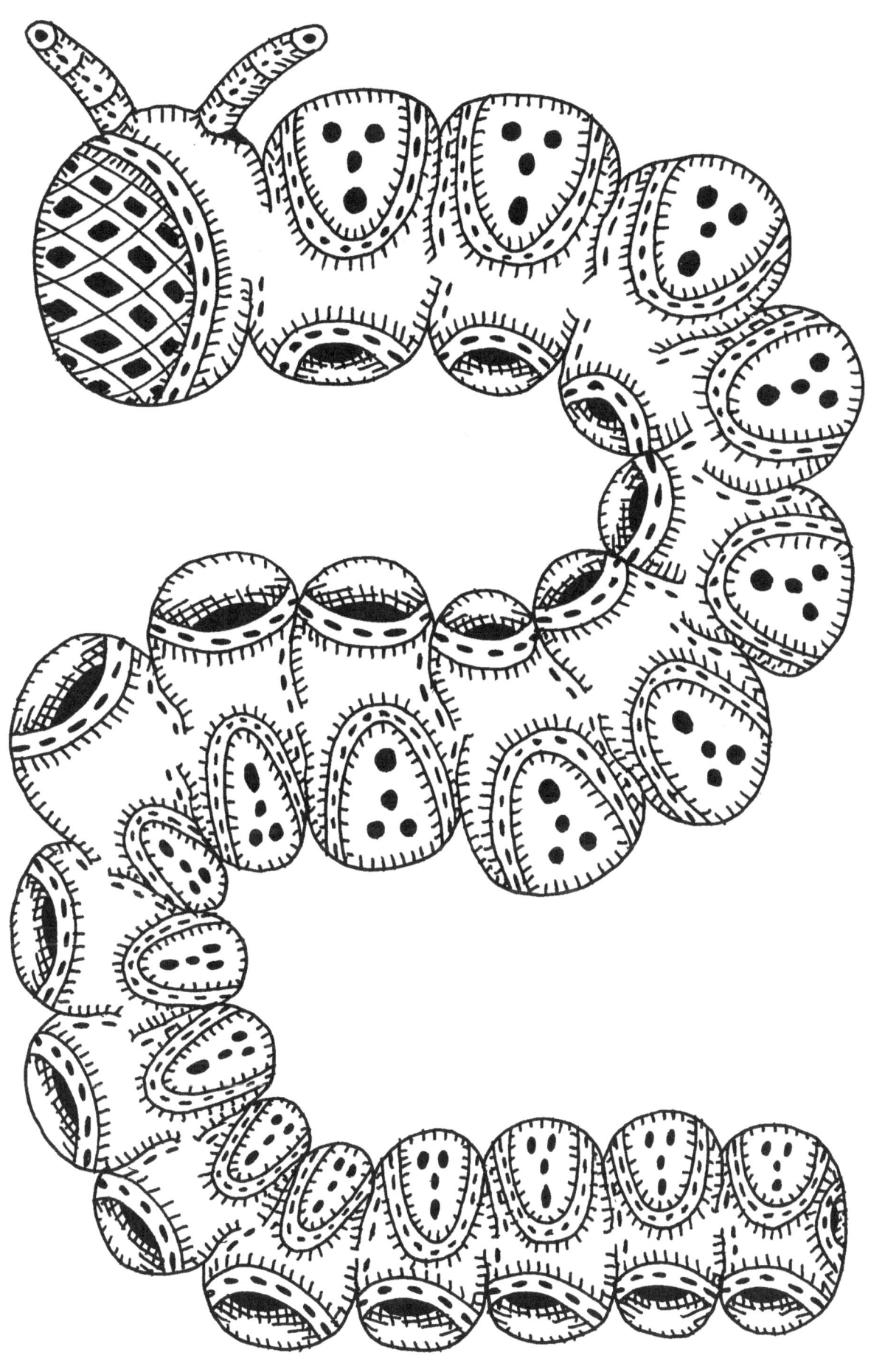

CATERPILLAR MULTI-BUG

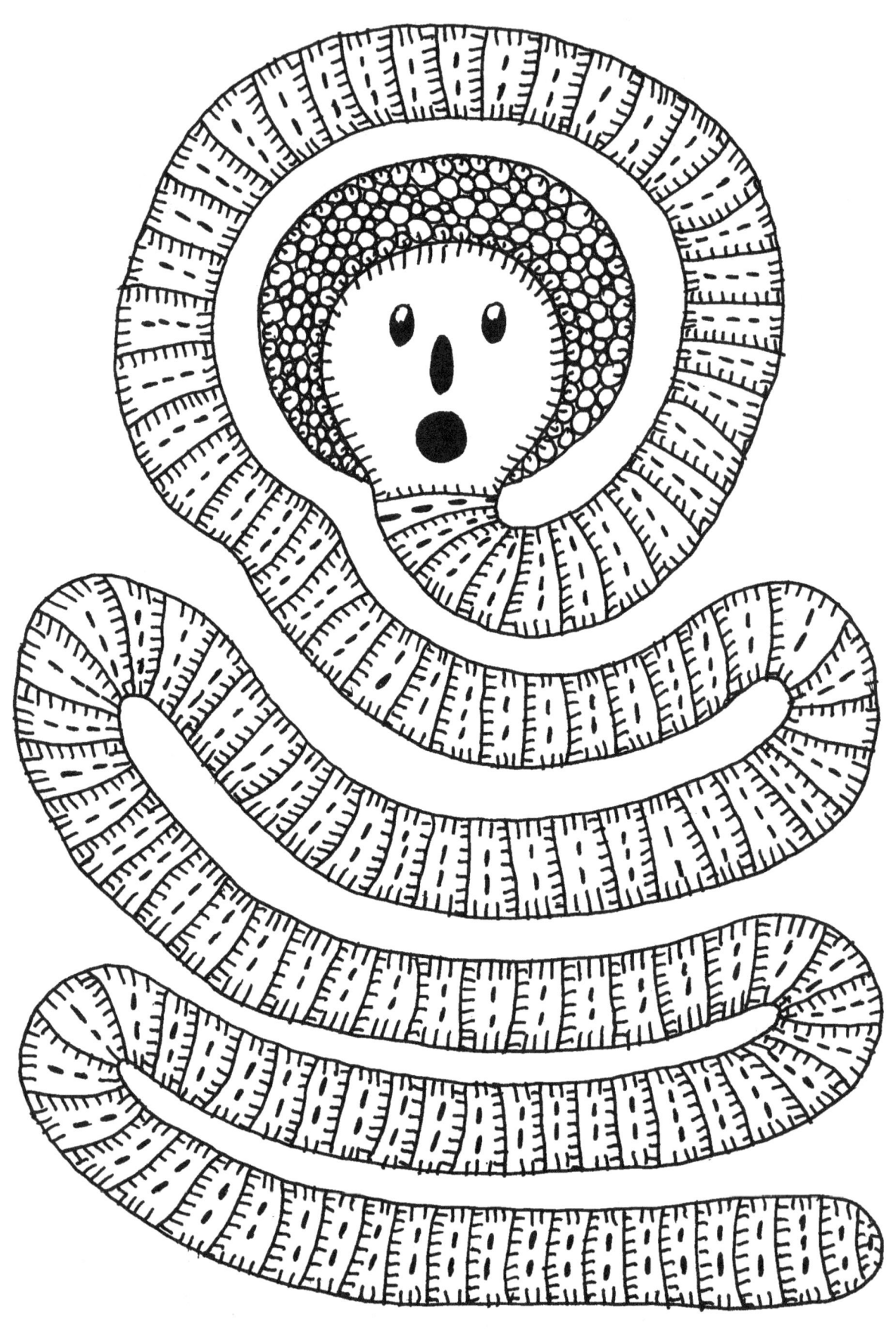

COILED BUBBLE-HEAD WORM

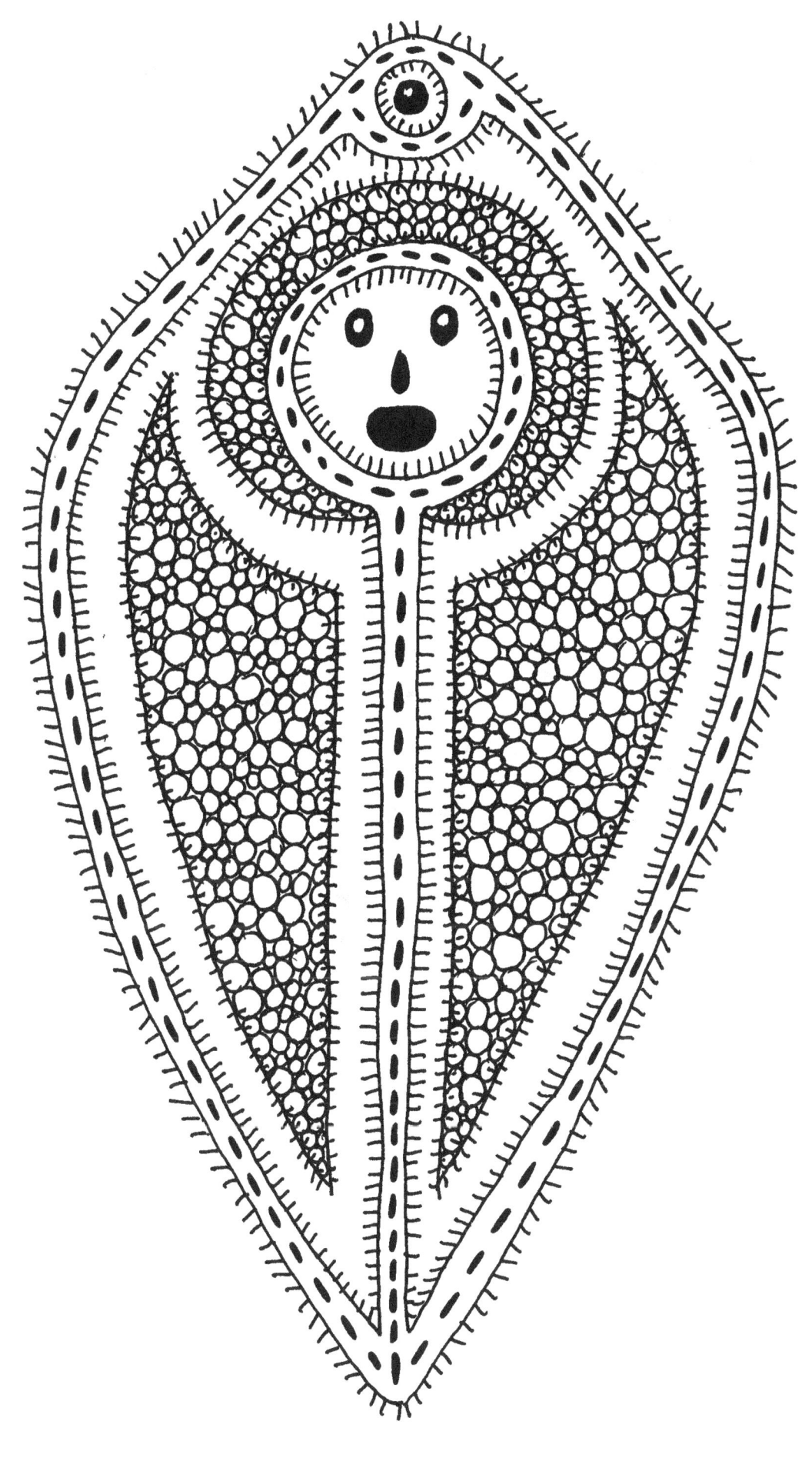

BUBBLE BUG

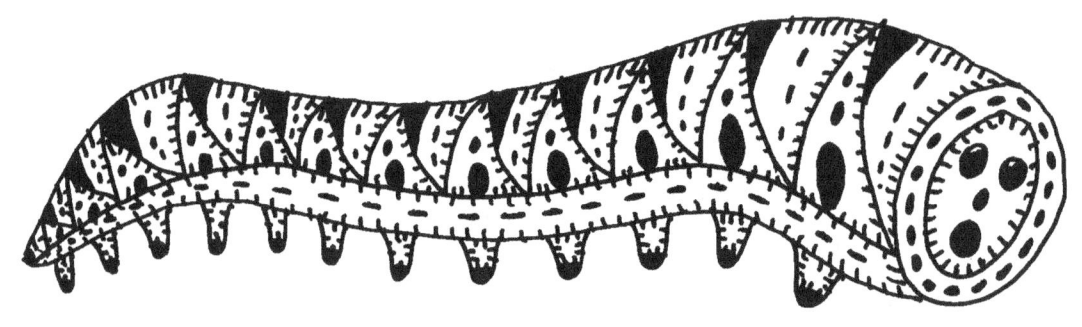

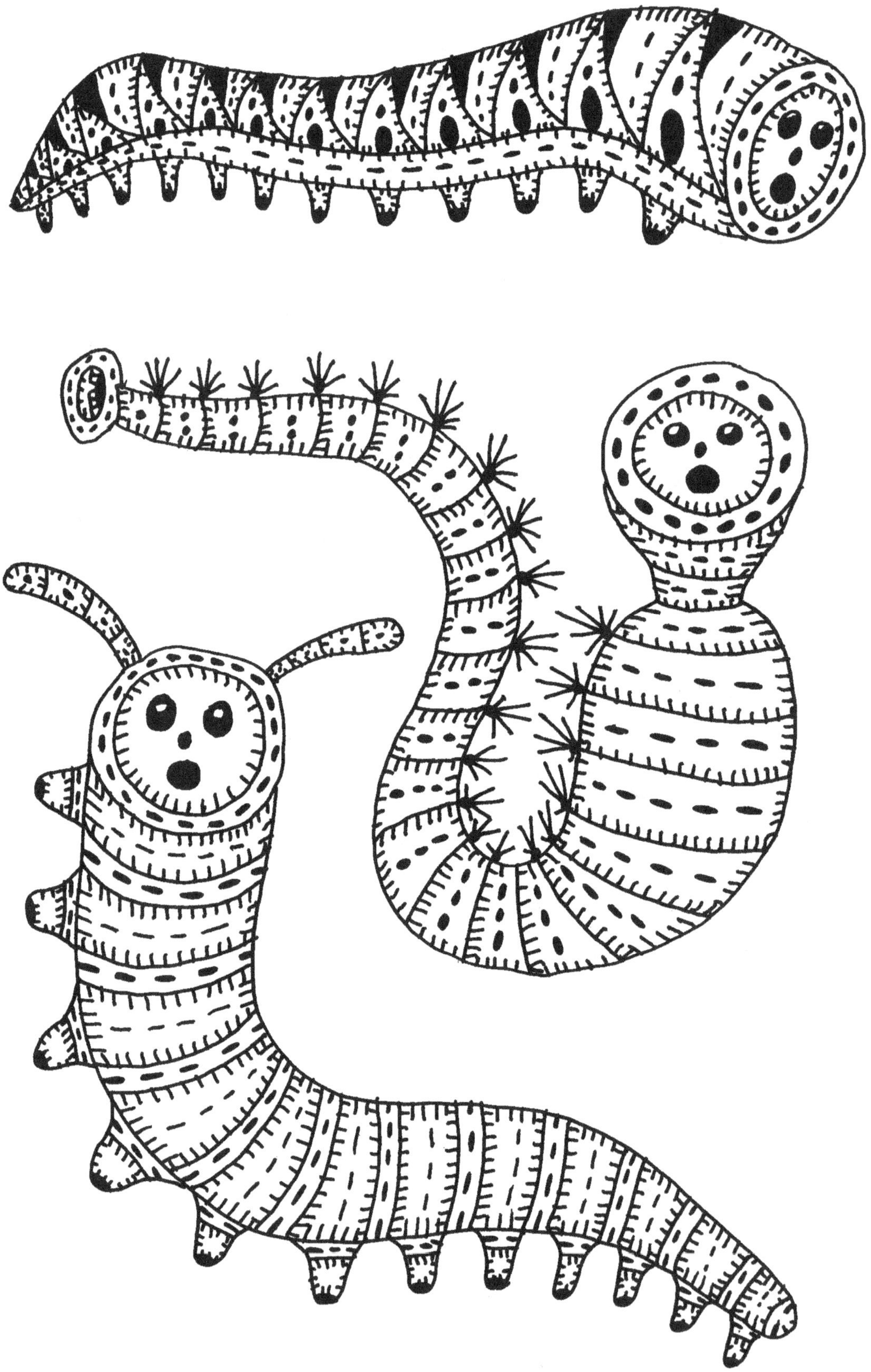

CRAWLING BUG VARIANTS

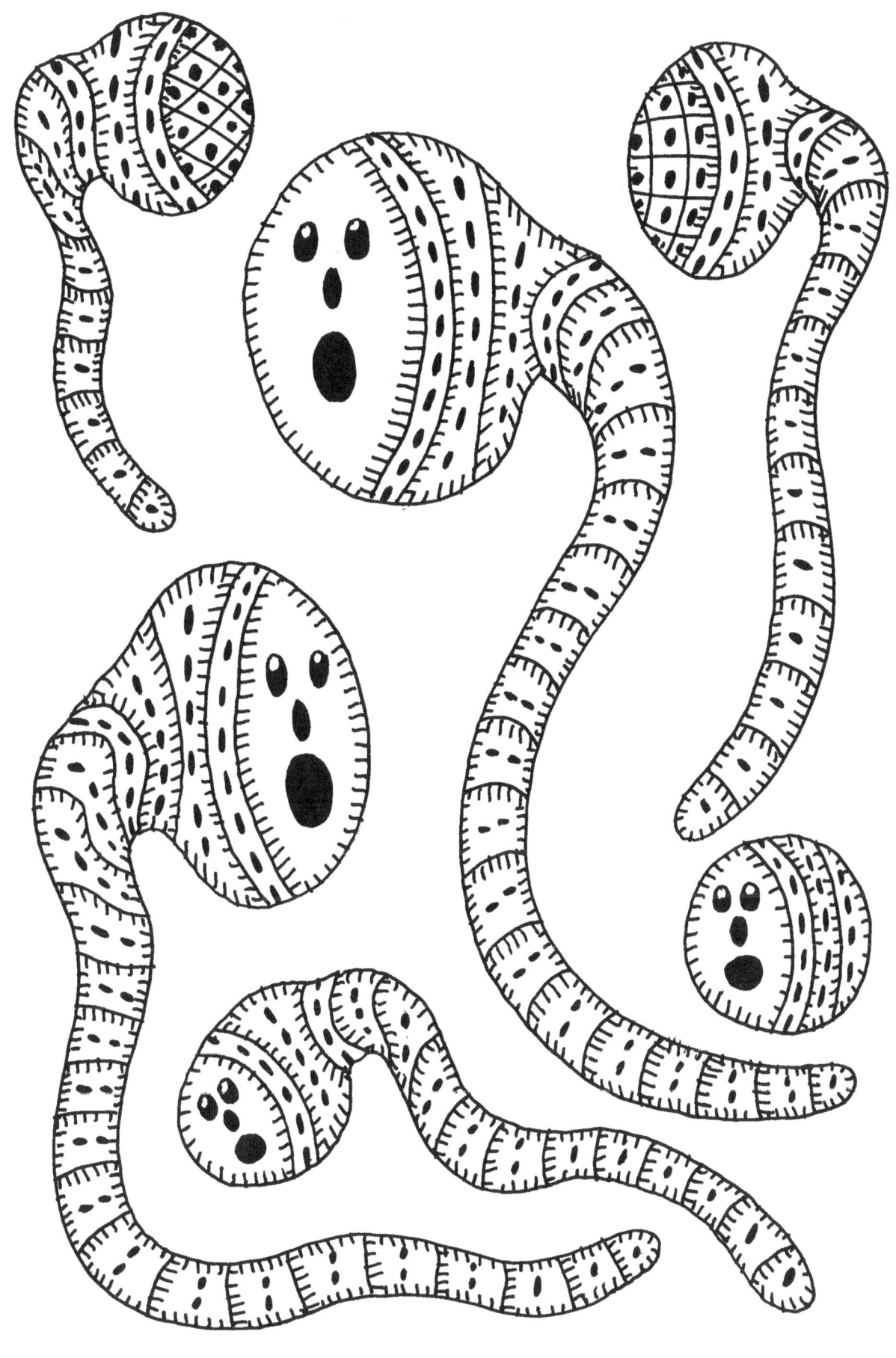

FUTURE-PRIMITIVE WORMS

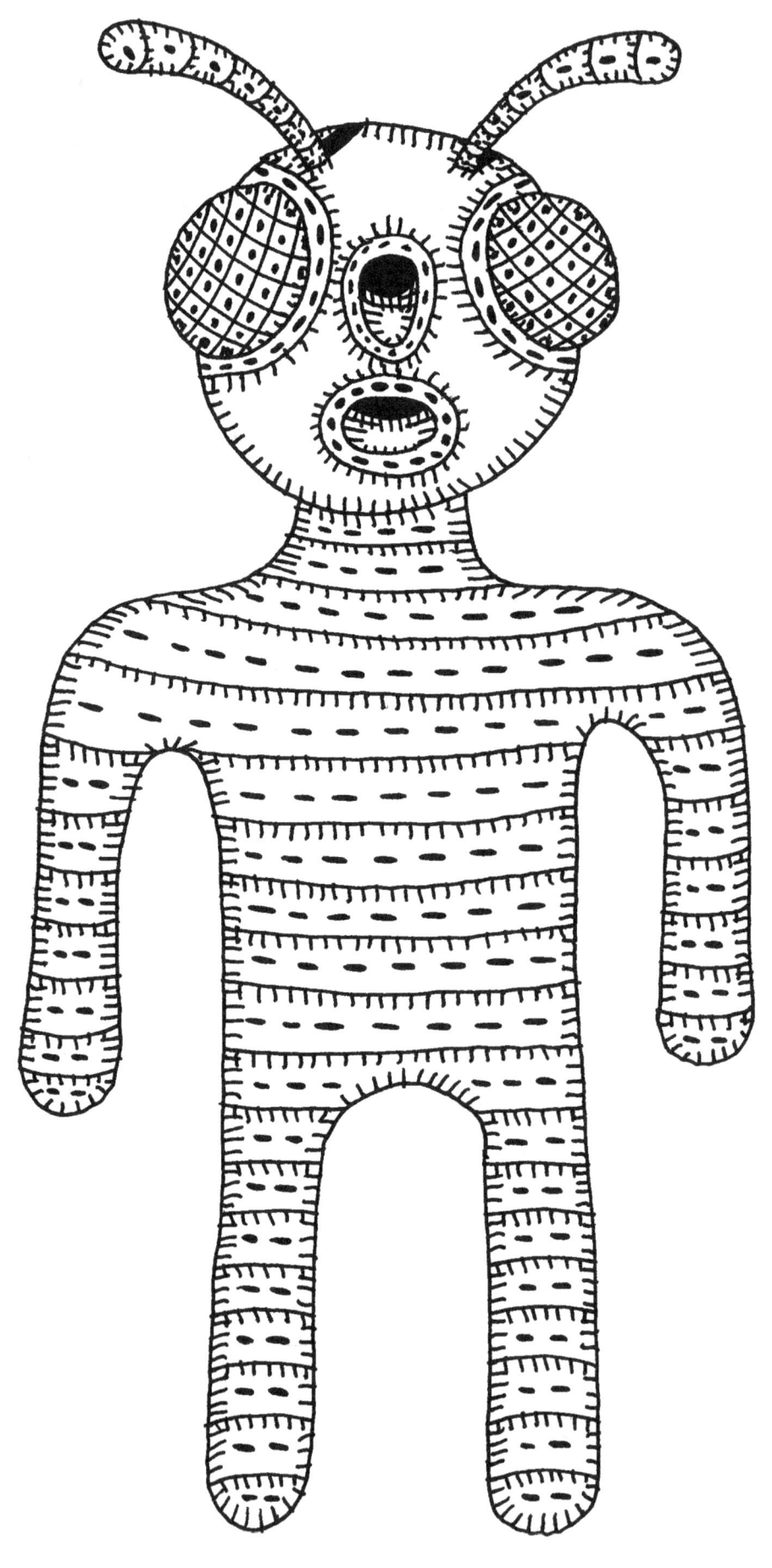

HUMANOID BUG

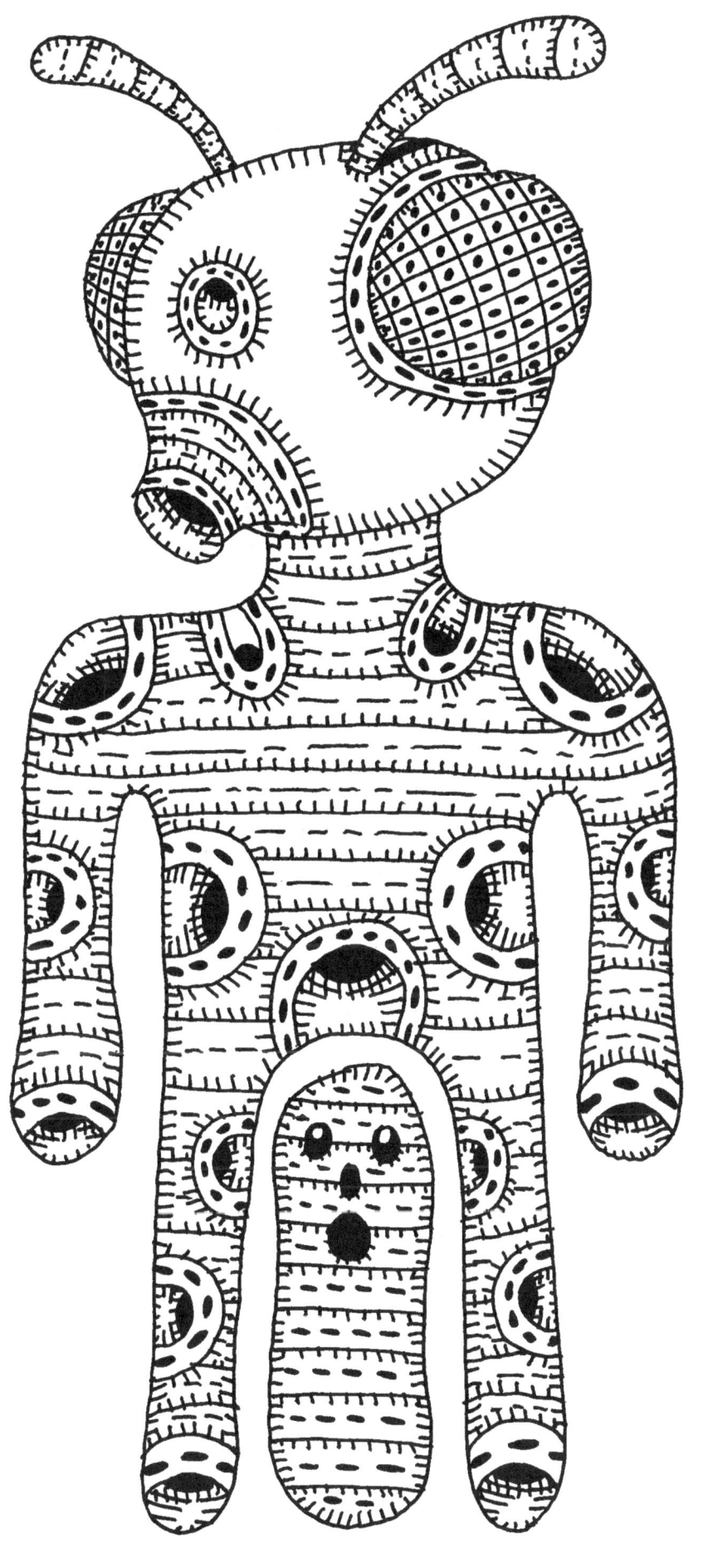

HUMANOID BUG SURVIVAL SUIT

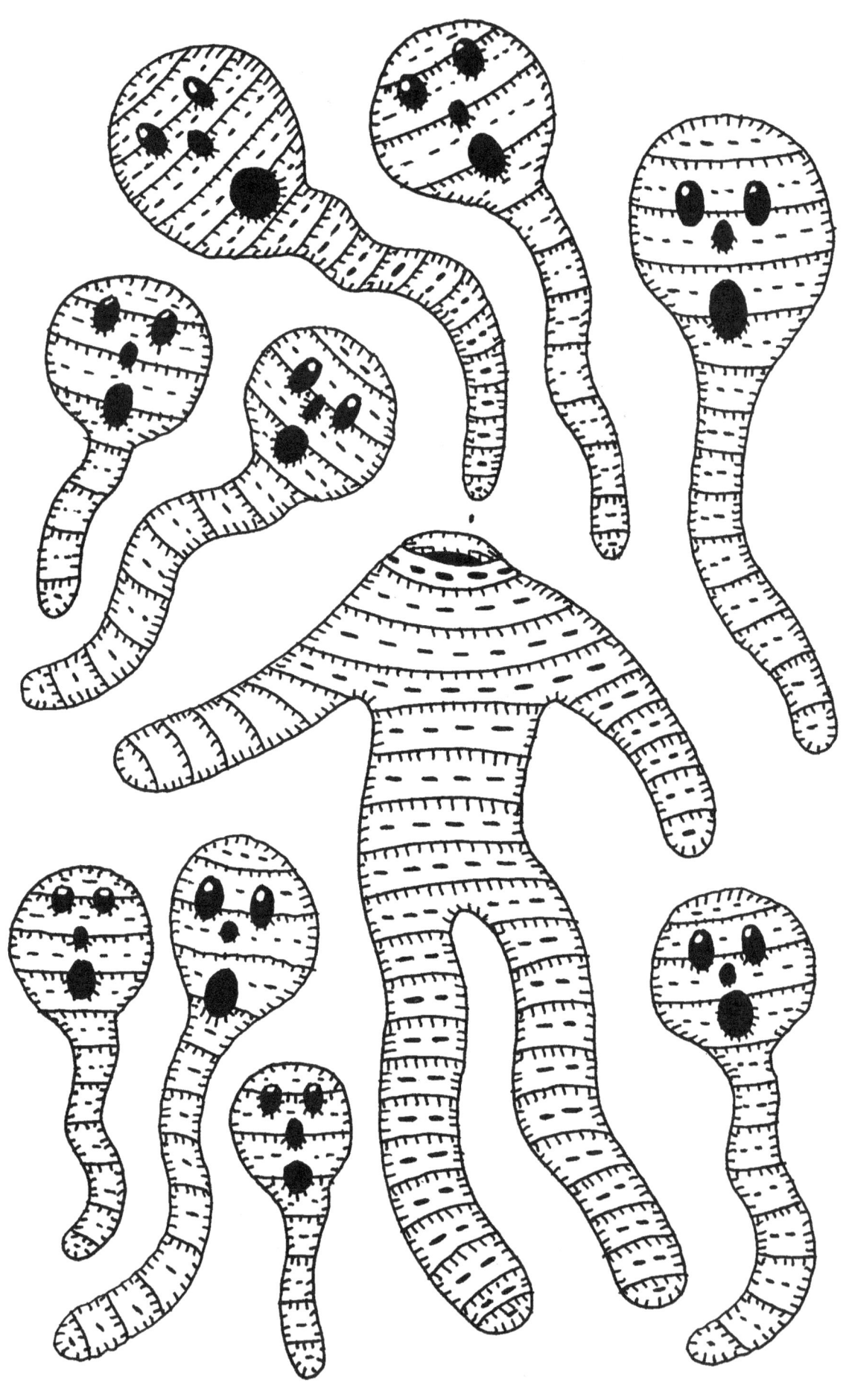

HUMANOID MUTATION

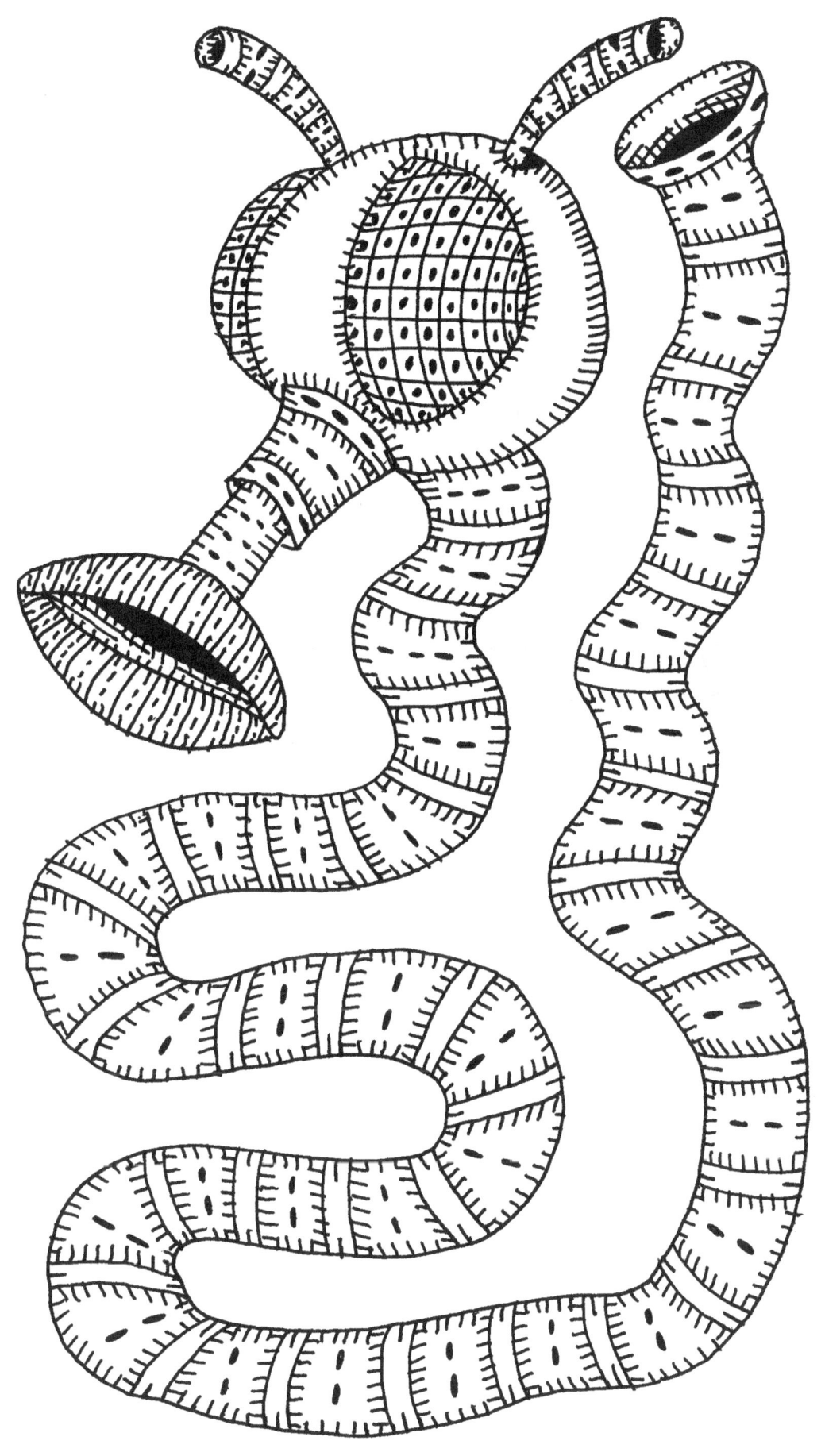

HYBRID TUBE BUG

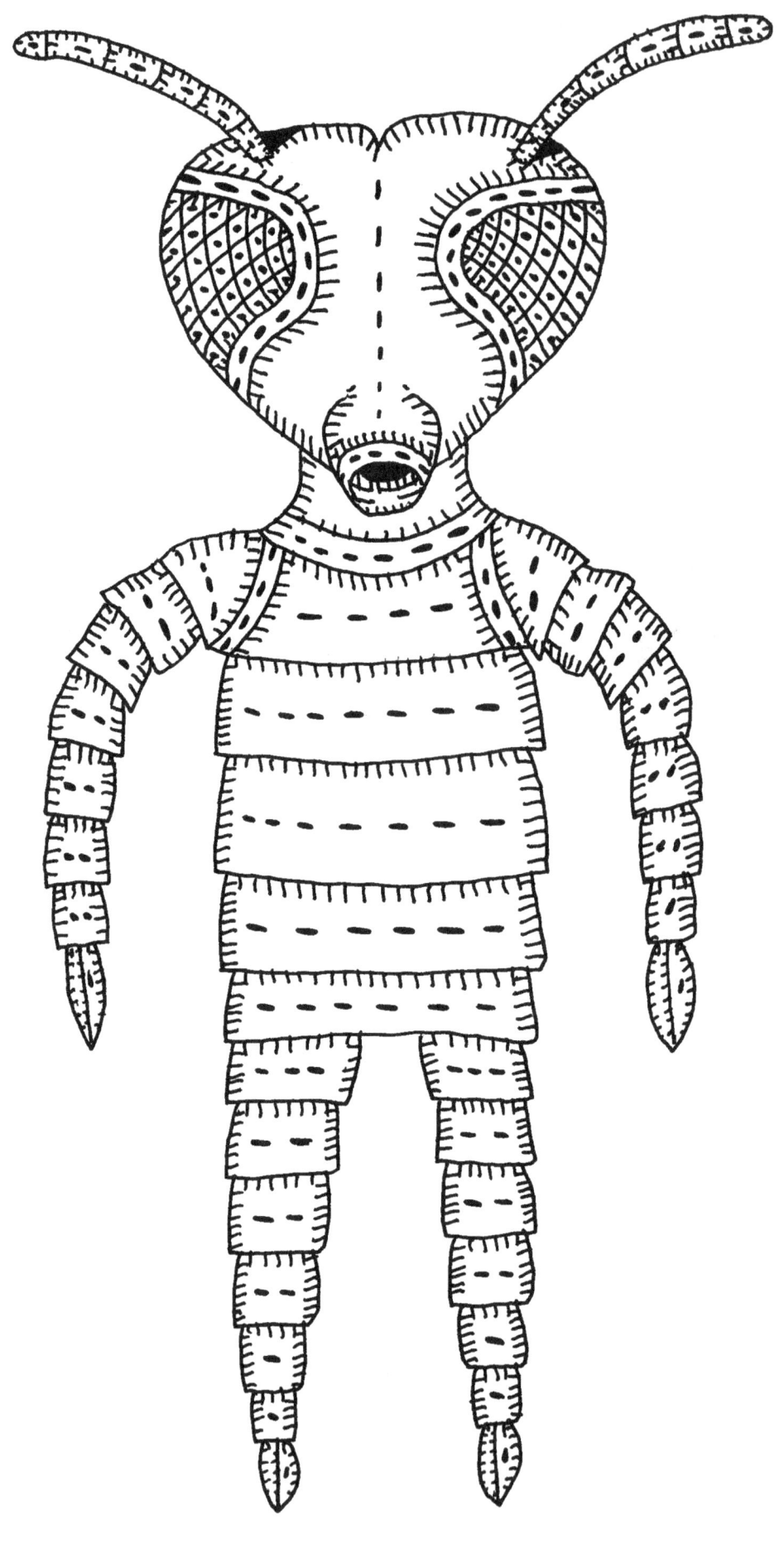

INSECTOID

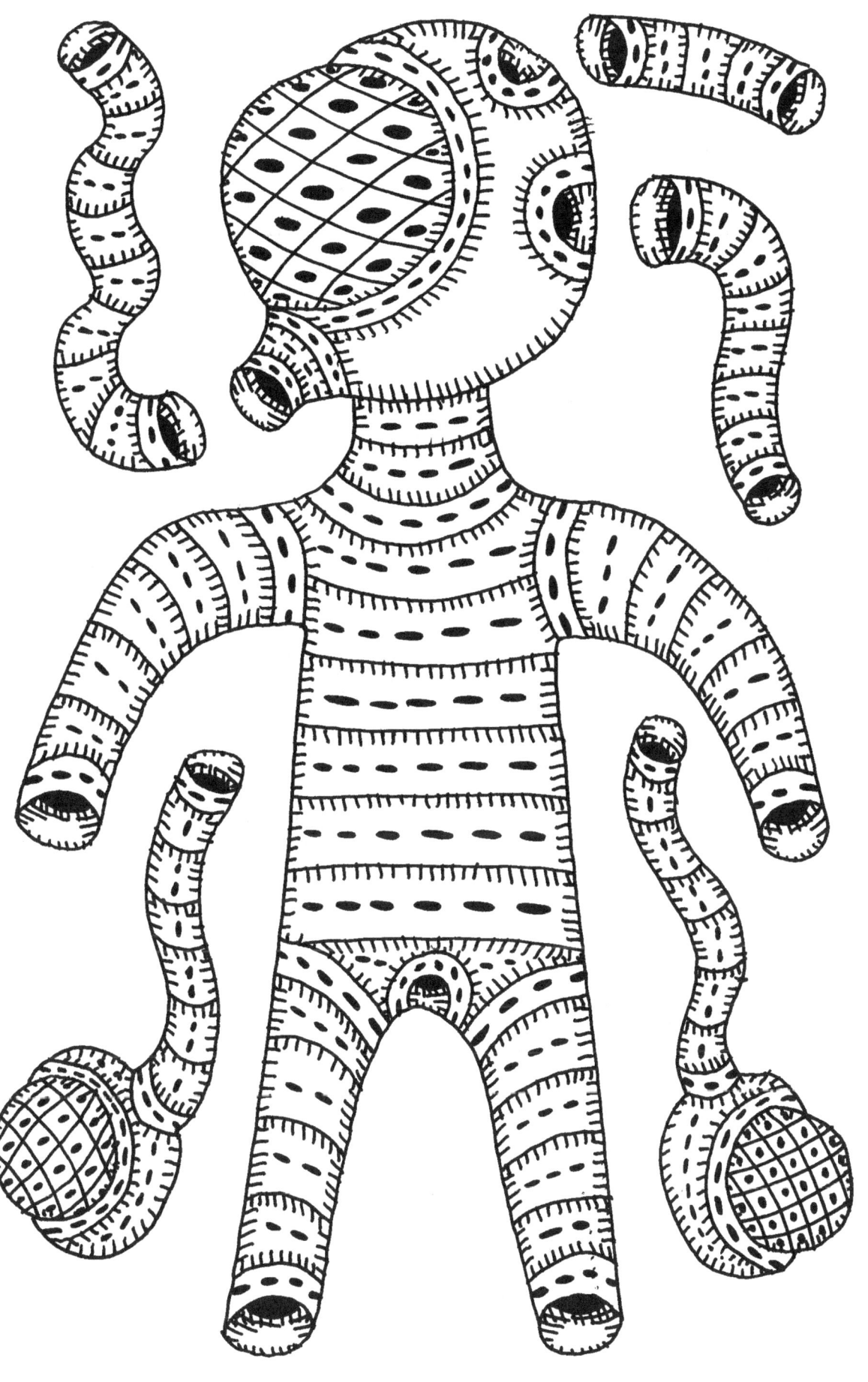

INSECTOID ADAPTATIONS

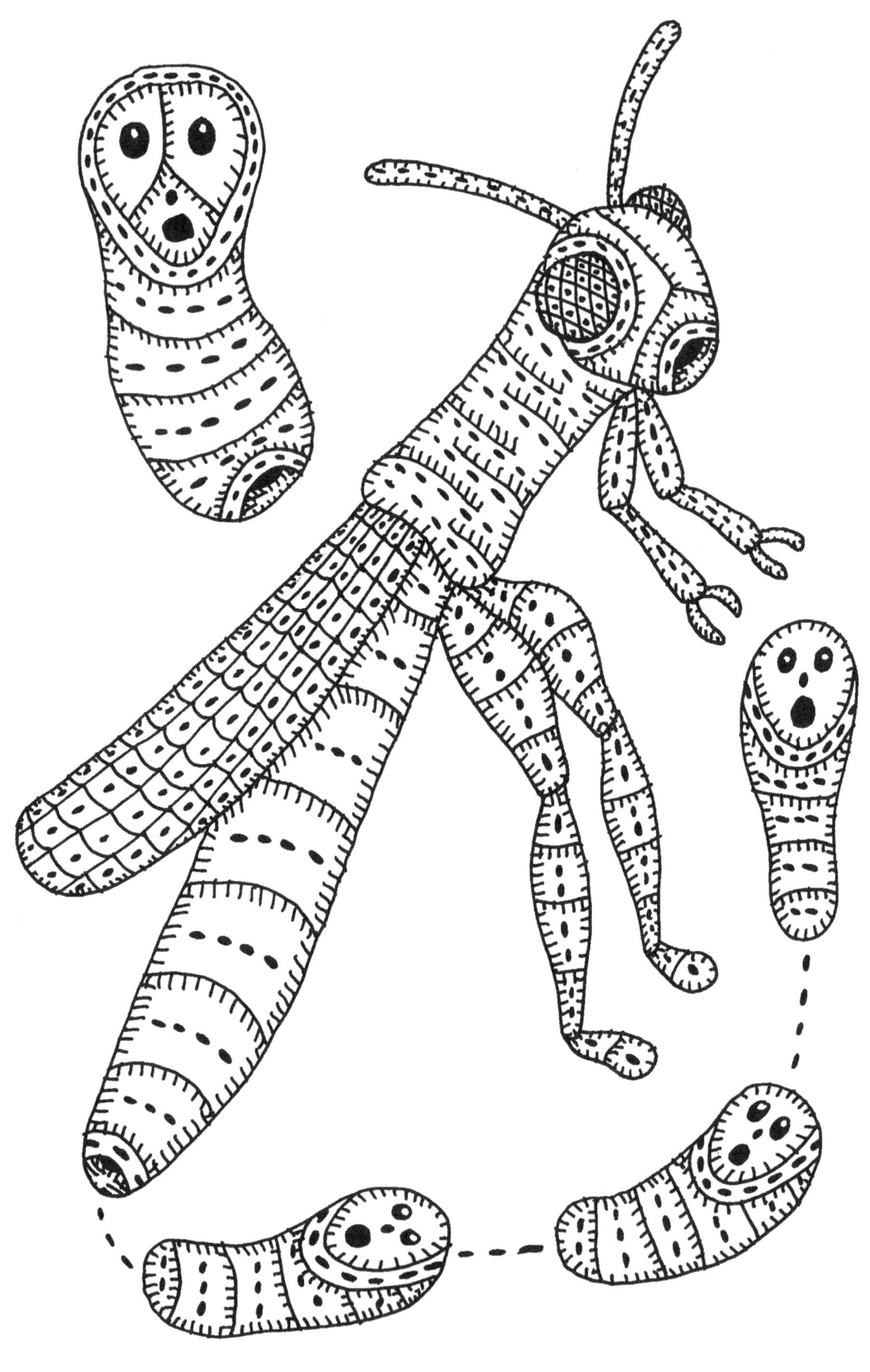

INSECT BROOD PRODUCTION

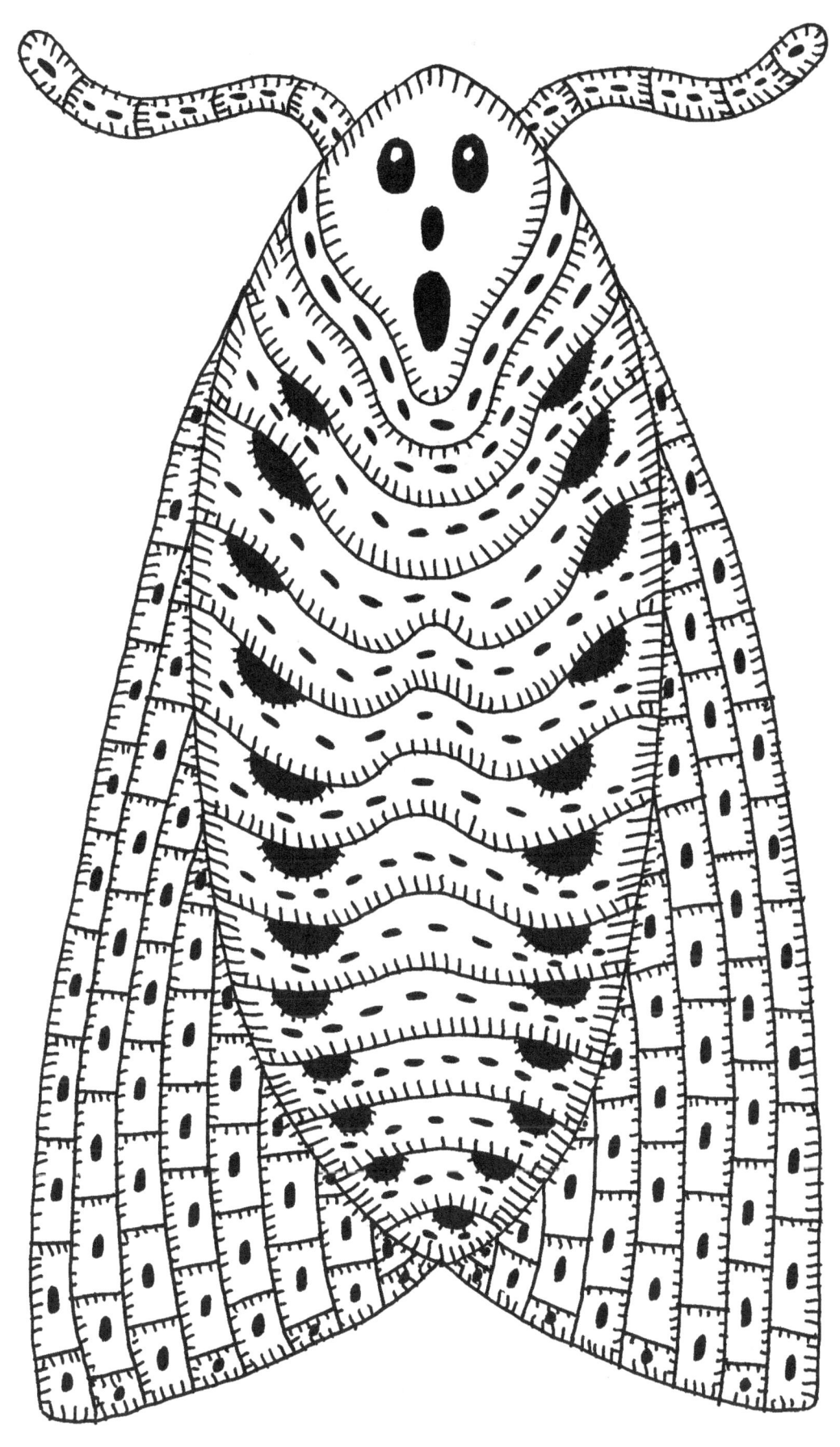

MOTH HYBRID

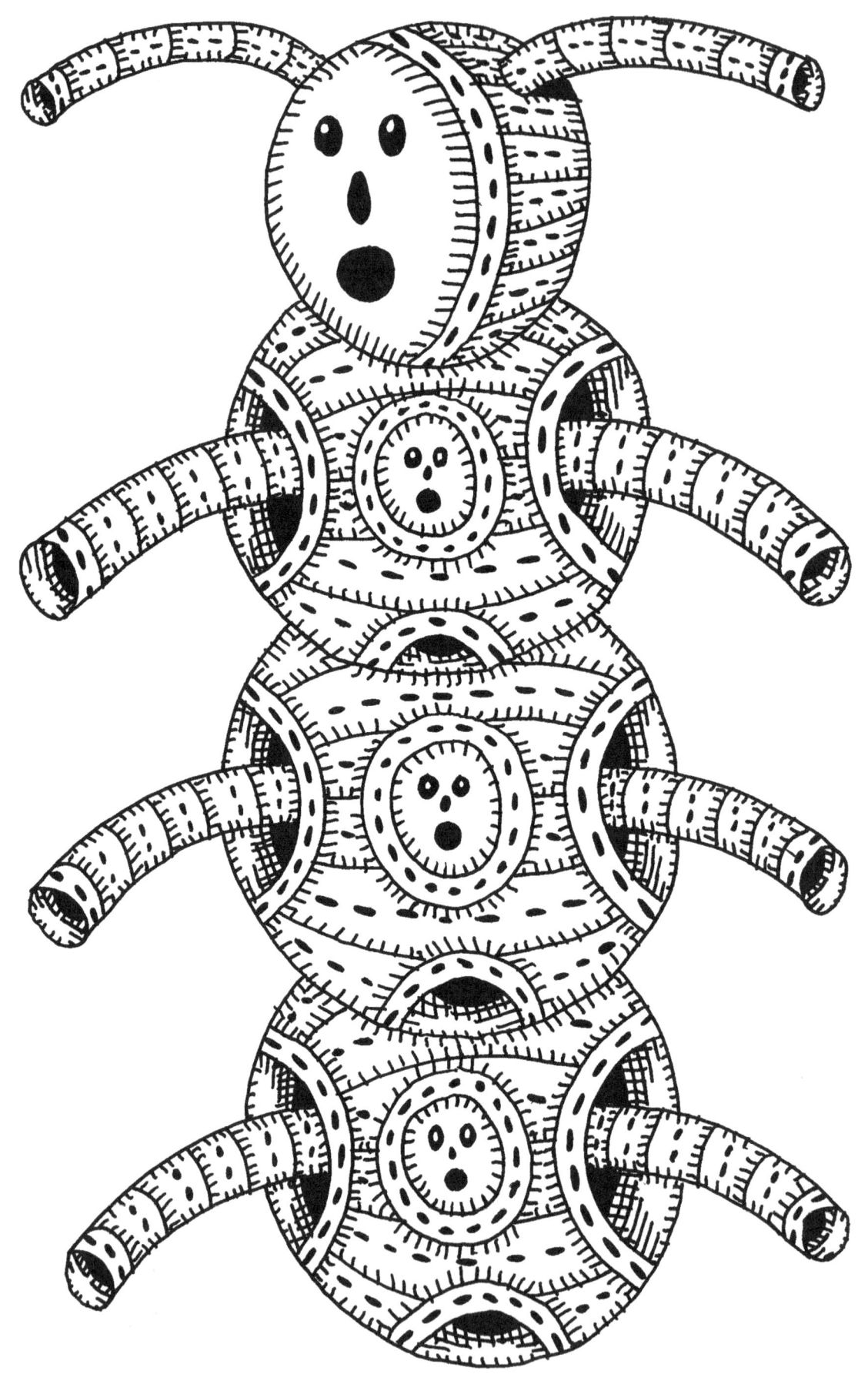

MOTHER BUG

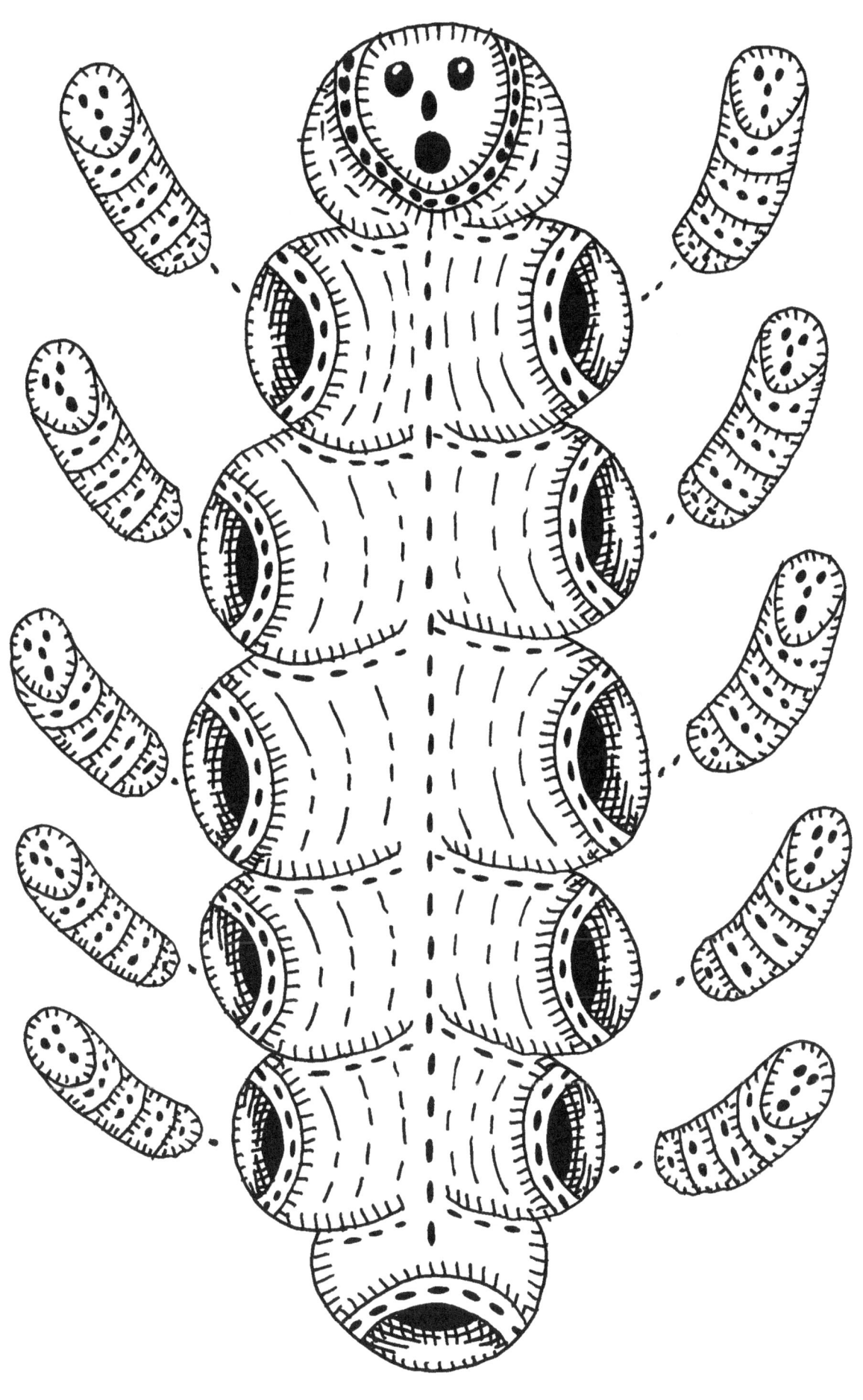

MOTHER BUG #2

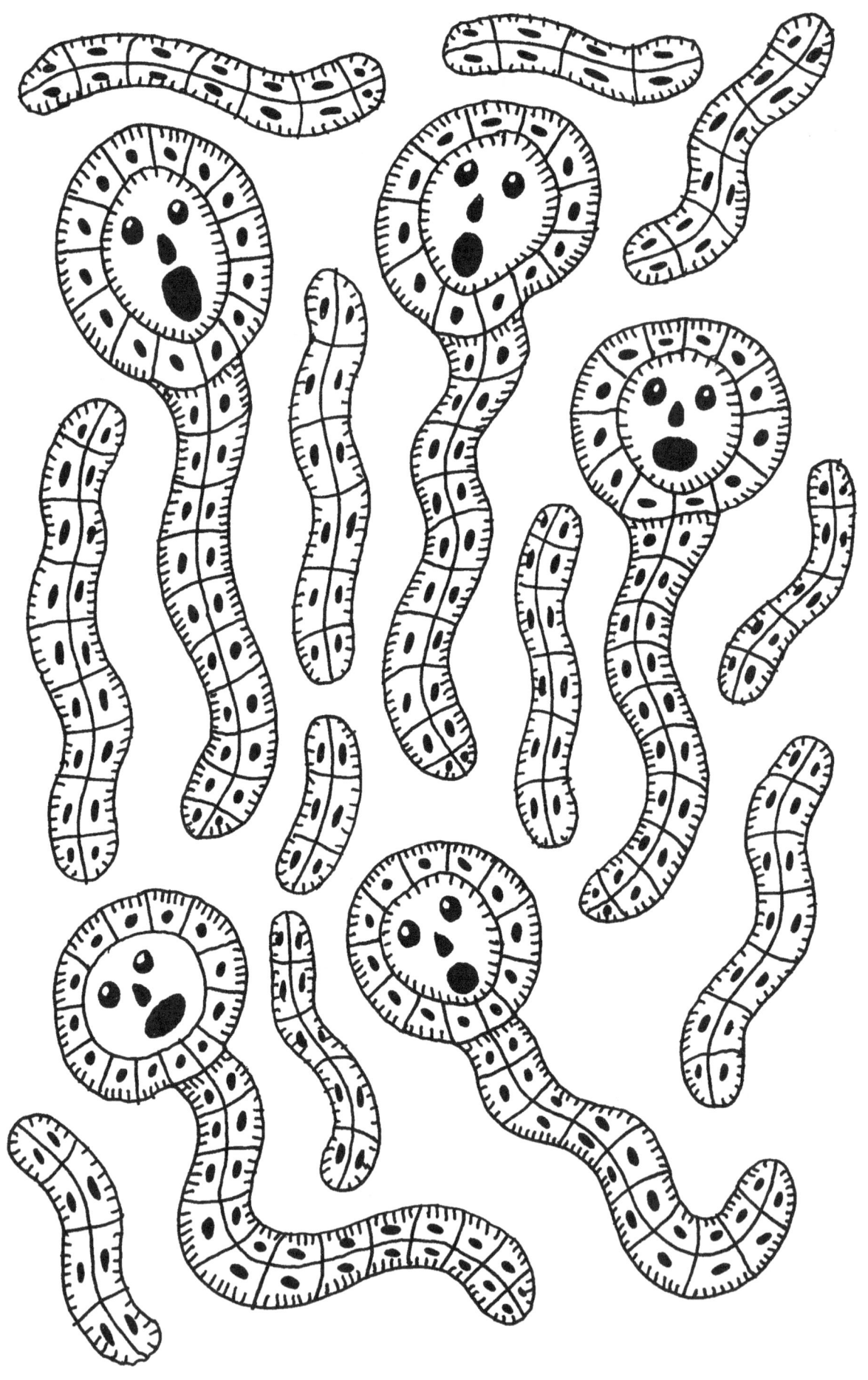

SPERM WORMS

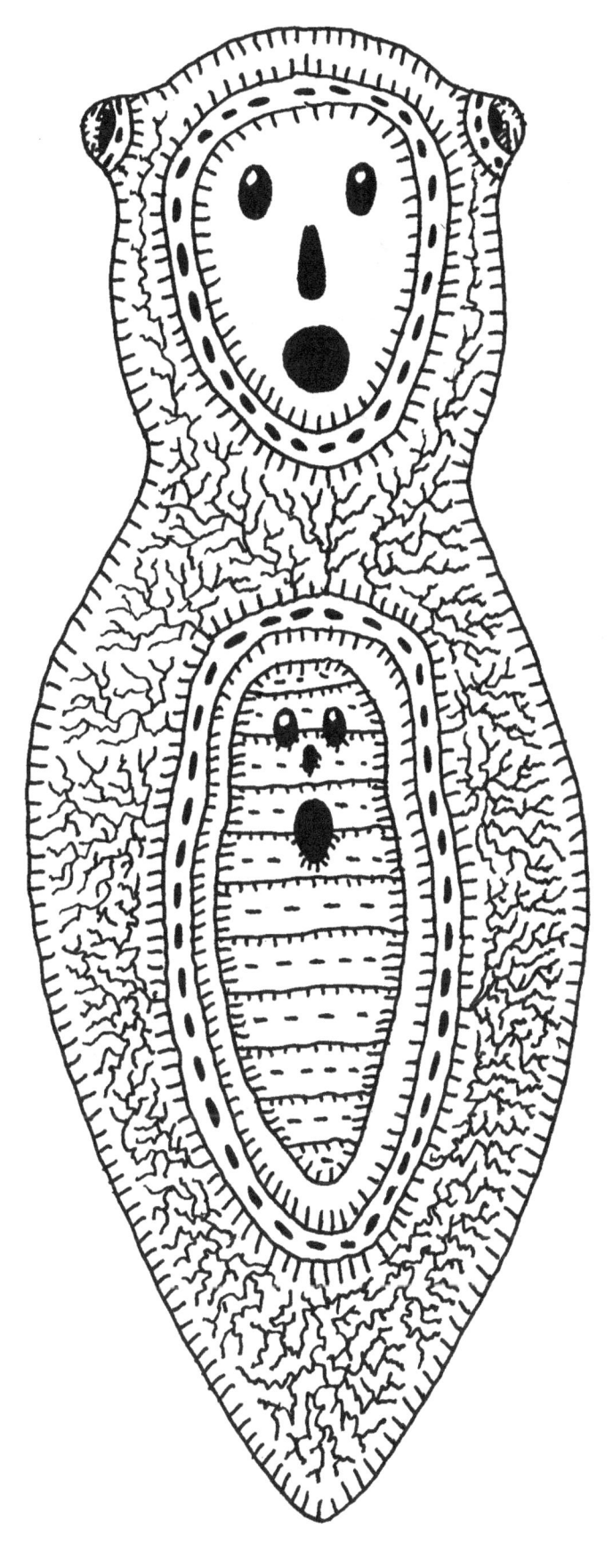

BLOOD-WORM PLACENTA

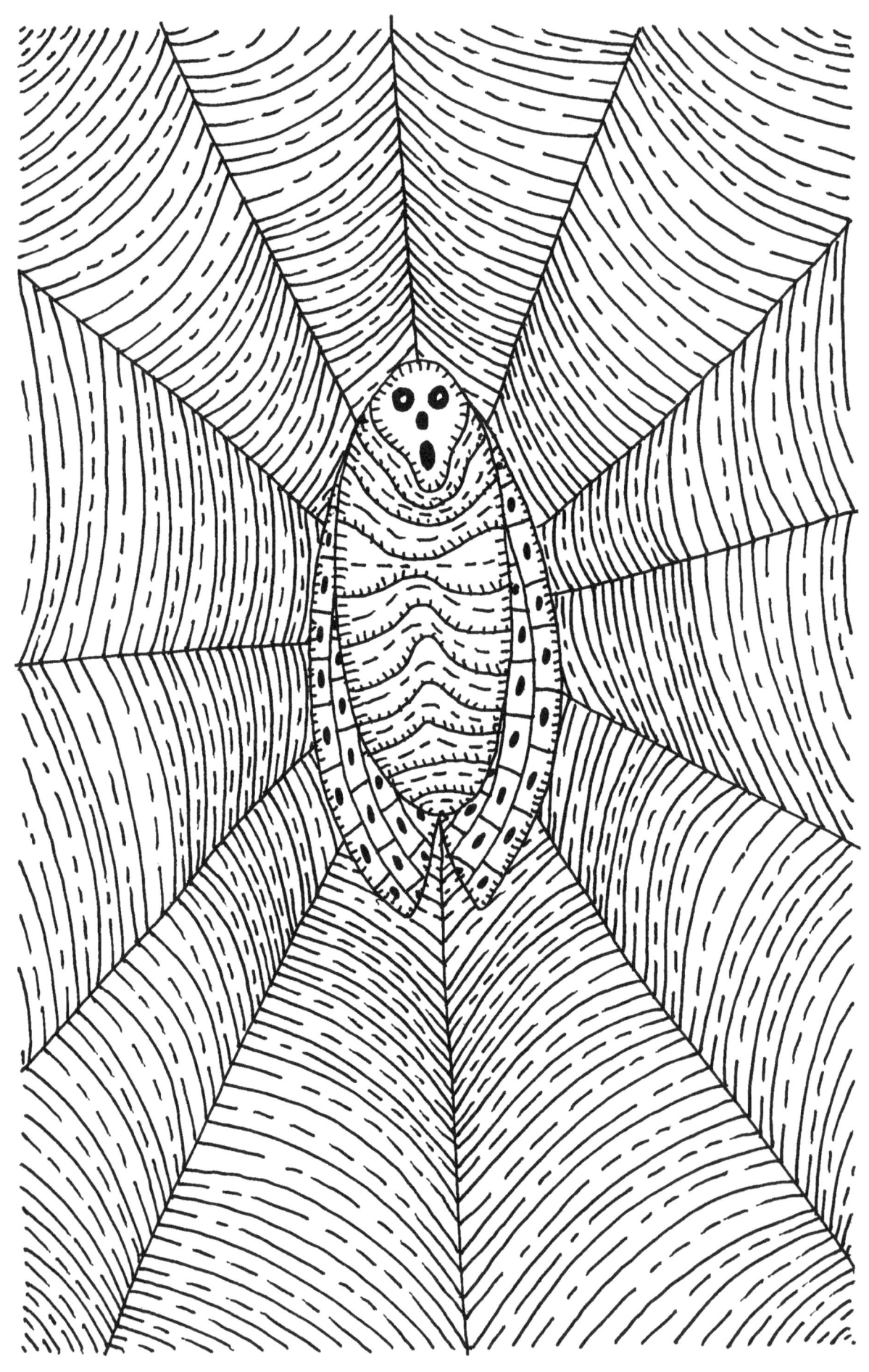

WEB PUPAE

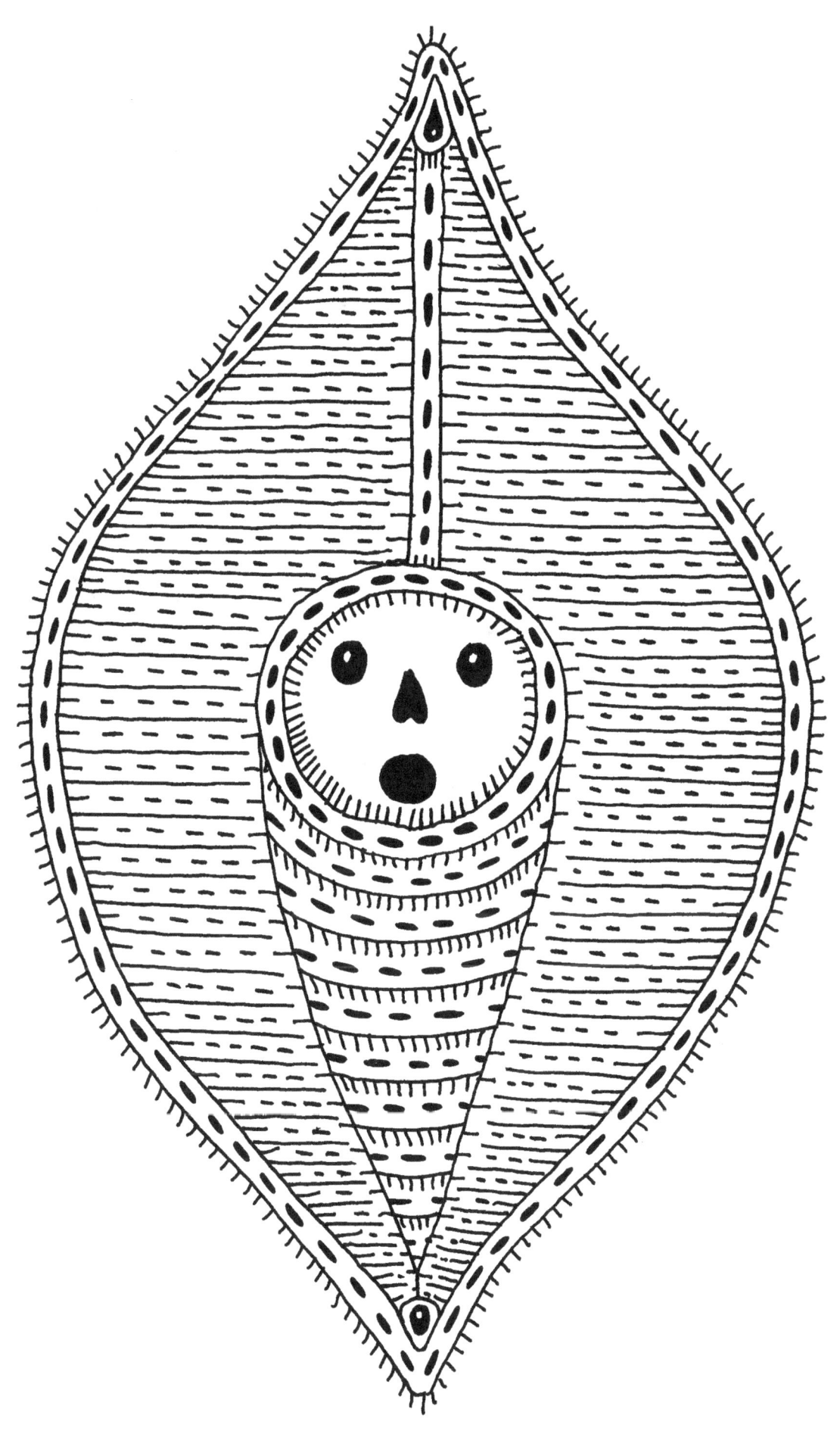

WORM HOLE

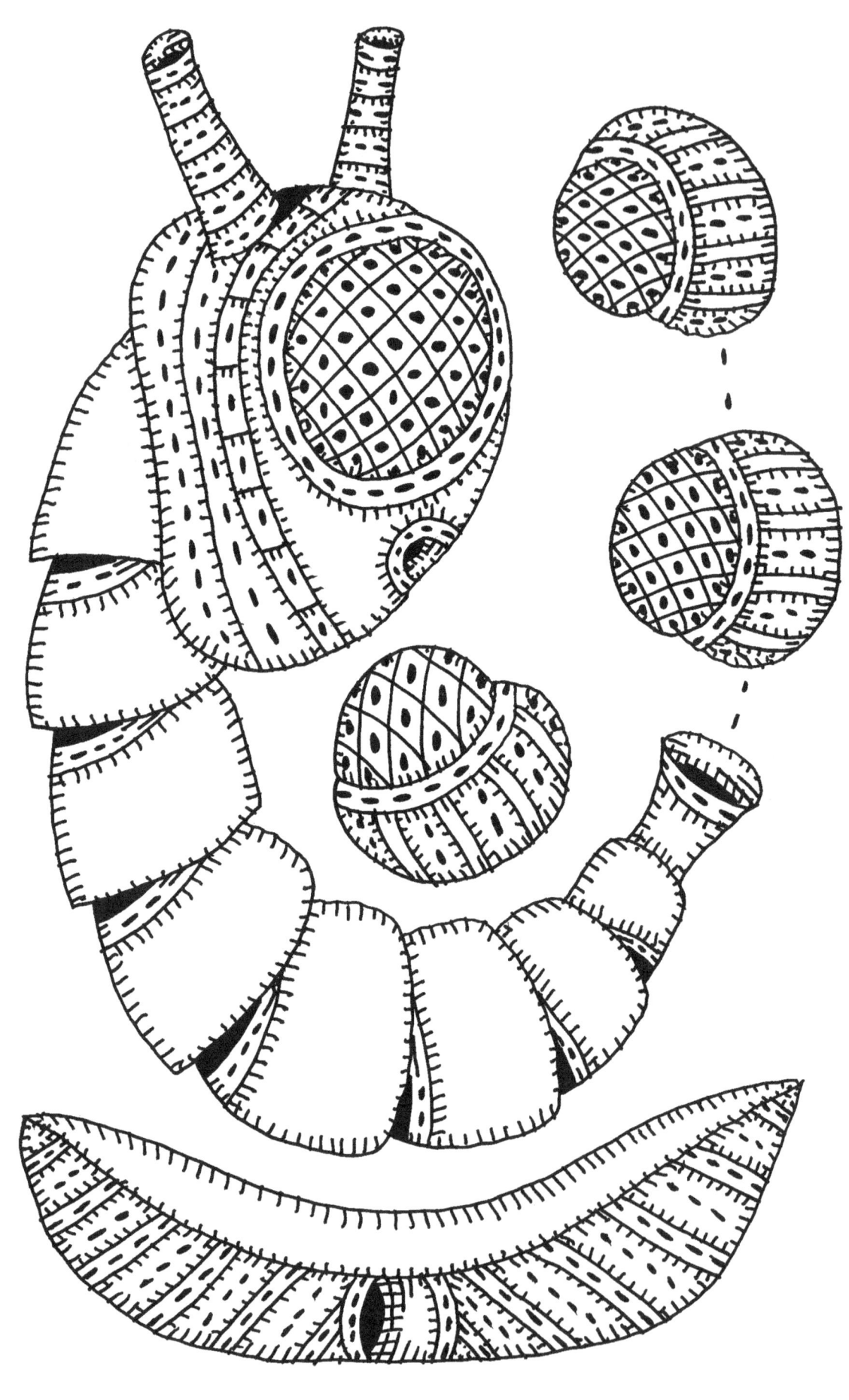

SENTINEL BUG PRODUCTION

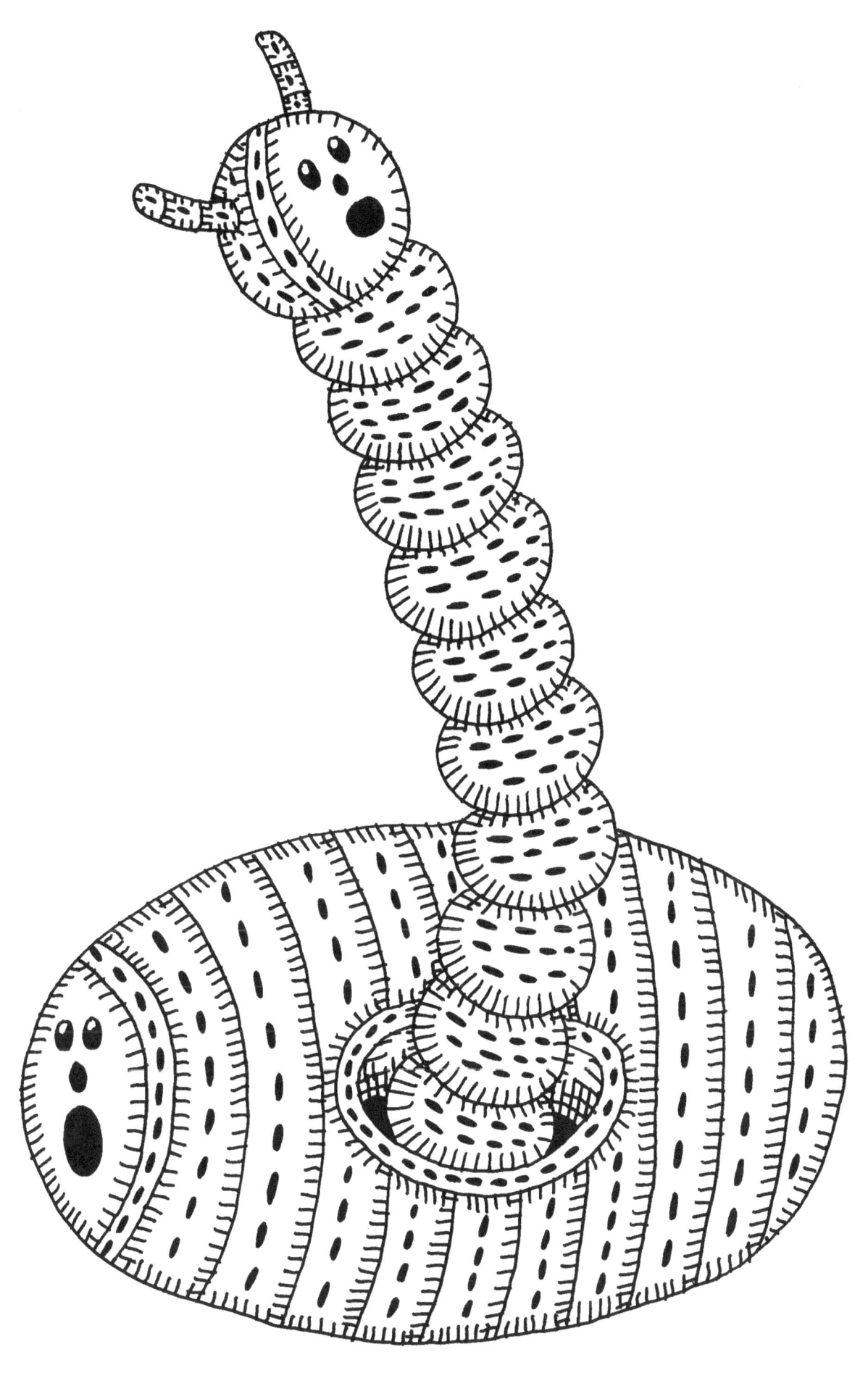

PARASITIC WORM

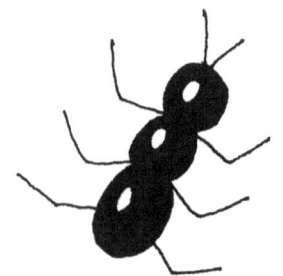

www.ingramcontent.com/pod-product-compliance
Lightning Source LLC
Chambersburg PA
CBHW081812220526
45468CB00007B/1821